6 TOP TRUMPS CARDS

FREE & EXCLUSIVE

INTENDED FOR MATURE AUDIENCES!

FAMILY GUY™

Pedigree

Published 2014. Pedigree Books Limited, Beech Hill House, Walnut Gardens, Exeter, Devon EX4 4DH.
www.pedigreebooks.com – books@pedigreegroup.co.uk
The Pedigree trademark, email and website addresses, are the sole and exclusive properties of Pedigree Group Limited, used under licence in this publication.

CONTENTS

"HOW DELIGHTFULLY AWFUL"

WELCOME TO THE FAMILY GUY ANNUAL 2015...

"YOU THINK ALL THIS GOODWILL JUST FALLS FROM THE FREAKIN' SKY? WELL, IT DOESN'T! IT FALLS OUT OF MY HOLLY JOLLY BUTT!"

- Lois (A Very Special Family Guy Freakin' Christmas)

In the words of Glenn Quagmire Esquire: "Allllriiiight!"

If you're opening this on Christmas Day, you lucky thing...Hope you're having the kind of "holly jolly" time Lois would be proud of.

If you picked it up in the sales – got yourself a little bargain – we're not judging. Well done.

Or, if you 'won' it, years from now, in an online auction: congratulations! You have excellent taste. And, like Stewie, you have just successfully travelled back in time…

All eyes are on Brian this year, as we glimpse into the headline-creating events from Season 12. We also take a look back at his life in showbiz and his very best bits - plus, of course, that special dog/baby friendship. Tissues at the ready: it's going to be emotional.

But that's not all… Tear yourself away from your phone – we bring you social networking, Griffin-style. We get into the festive spirit, with a look back at holidays past. There's a touch of class, with the great and good of Hollywood gracing these very pages, as we present our pick of the Coolest Cameos in Family Guy. Test your knowledge of the show – and your favourite songs – with our quizzes. Oh, and find out once and for all, the answer to that big question: Which Griffin Are You? We know it's been keeping you awake at night.

If all this reading makes you hungry, turn to page 27, for a handy – and very tasty – 'Road to...' themed recipe. And, if for some reason you get an unmentionable itch, like Peter, make a "Butt Scratcher" on page 37. We think of everything.

Enjoy!

Family Guide:

Discover what's new in Quahog for 2015...

PETER

He's the daddy. He's also the work-shirking, prank-loving, chicken-fighting buffoon; the big kid who never quite grew up. What "the fat one" lacks in intellect, he makes up for in enthusiasm. Tons of it.

Peter may not be the smartest cookie, but he's on a self-improvement mission in Season 12. You can find out more about this, look at his school days – and, more importantly, see the photos! – on page 20. And talking of cookies, they are the focus of Peter and Lois' brand new business, in new episode, Baking Bad. Sweet, huh?

Also this season: Peter's taking up a filthy habit to get out of work, discovering he has a very tiny twin and figuring out the cause of his recent (and terrible) "Dad breath". Read more about all of this, in our Season 12 Episode Guide, from page 54.

LOIS

Formerly Lois Patrice Pewterschmidt, born into a life of privilege, the now Mrs. Griffin gave it all up for the love of one (very gassy) man. Yep, that's Peter. She even turned down a gift of ten million dollars from her folks. Ten million! Talk about keeping it real.

She is a born romantic, and this season, in Boopa-dee Bappa-dee, she convinces Peter to take a trip to Italy, on a mission to put the spark back into their marriage (Or just plain cons him into it). Get a sneaky peek at their dolce vita on page 58.

Lois has some serious skills. We're taking a look back at her (Not-So) Hidden Talents on page 22 – where there's a reminder, if ever it were needed, to NEVER get on the wrong side of Carter and Barbara's eldest daughter.

BRIAN

He's the martini-swiggin', novel-writin', swing-singin', Lois-lovin', road-trippin' Canine Griffin – and you don't always appreciate what you've got until it's gone.

Season 12 is a big one for Brian, as you are no doubt already aware. Prepare for the emotional floodgates to open, in Life of Brian (and read more about the episode on page 59).

What would the Griffins – and the rest of us – do without Brian? Sure, he can sometimes be a bit of a douche, but, to paraphrase Stewie, he's OUR douche. We take a look back at his life on page 48 and cast an eye over his literary endeavours on page 50.

Oh, and from page 24 there's a chance to relive the incredibly satisfying – and funny – journey that is Stewie and Brian's Road to Friendship.

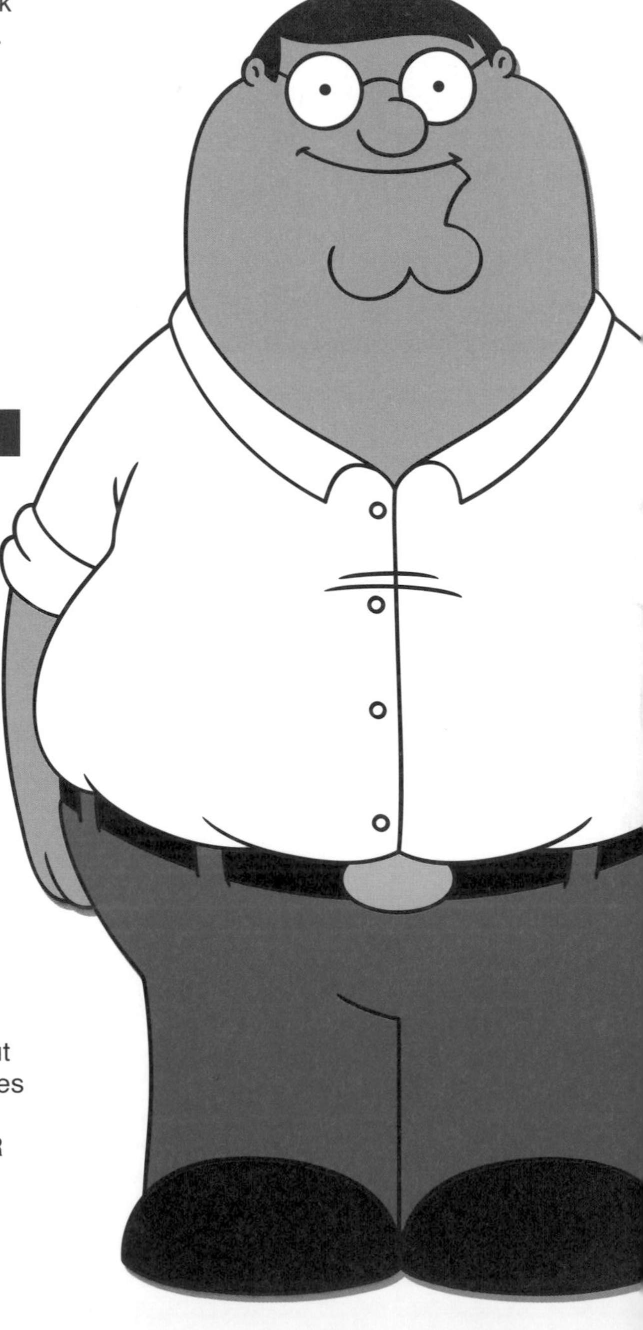

Peter: "We got a wonderful family."
Lois: "No we don't. There's Meg and Dummy and Bighead."

(Call Girl)

STEWIE

Once an evil genius, Stewie has mellowed somewhat. He may be very confused about his identity lately (particularly when it comes to the objects of his affections), but he is still the go-to chap for all your time-travelling needs.

In the brand new season, he's out to prevent his own birth – with alarming consequences – and he also has a very important mission on his hands, regarding his very special pal, "Bri".

If it's adventure you're after, Stewie is definitely your sidekick. Settle back for a song and dance – and prepare to save Christmas - in our 'Road to' special, on page 24. And the festivities continue in Christmas Guy, on page 61. And if you're after a colourful insult, of the old-school style, our one-year-old with the extensive vocabulary can, and most certainly will, oblige. Page 52 is where you need to head.

MEG

Poor Meg. Life has not been easy for her. All she ever wanted was to fit in, to be 'normal' – and, well, look where this has got her. Get ready to cringe, big time, on page 30, as we dare to remember her Most Mortifying Moments.

In the very first season, Peter said to her, "listen Meg, you're a one-of-a-kind girl with a mind of her own – you see, that's what people hate... Just be the girl you think everyone else wants you to be." (Chitty Chitty Death Bang)

Meg's taken these words a bit too fully to heart, but perhaps – shock horror! – Peter isn't the best at the life-advice? This season – in Meg Stinks! (page 71) – she's finally bonding with her dad (and not in secret, this time). She's also taking on the high school psychopath, with a bit of help from Quagmire, in A Fistful of Meg (page 57).

CHRIS

The biggest Griffin boy may have taken after his pop in the intellect stakes, but rare moments of genius occasionally shine through. (Like a flashlight through his ears...) We give you his Wit and Wisdom on page 32.

If awkward were an academic subject, Chris would get straight A's. But Chris is striking it lucky this season, with lots of interest from the girls – particularly in Baby Got Black (page 70).

The focus is also on Chris in brand new episode, Secondhand Spoke (page 67), when he and Stewie embark on a bit of brotherly bonding. And he's spending quality time with his Grandpa Pewterschmidt, and unwittingly inheriting his fortune, in Fresh Heir (page 66).

QUAGMIRE

One word for you: "Giggity". It's good to have a hobby. But if you thought Quagmire only had one thing on his mind, think again. There's another side to Quahog's pervy pilot, and he's letting slip his robe of sex-pestery, on page 46, to reveal his (Very Random) Acts of Kindness.

There are dark times ahead for Quagmire. As he says to Meg in Season 12, he knows a thing or two about the limits of the human body. But he's about to find out his boundaries, and this time, he's not calling the shots... Read more about Quagmire's Quagmire on page 56. Oh, and did you know that Quagmire has his own secretary, Shirley? Meg stumbles across his "base of operations", in A Fistful of Meg (page 57).

JOE

He's the self-proclaimed "intense wheelchair guy" (The Giggity Wife), and Joe's friendship with Peter has developed considerably, since he first arrived on Spooner Street, with son Kevin, wife Bonnie and daughter Susie in baby bump form (possibly the longest pregnancy in the history of, well, pregnancy).

Remember Joe's heroic Christmas story? That's laid bare as the work of fiction it truly was, in Festive Family Guy, on page 12. There, we also remember the work of his alter ego, "Joe Swansonson".

Joe's convincing Peter to broaden his mind, in brand new episode, The Most Interesting Man in the World (page 69), and he's also revealing what he and Bonnie get up to in their spare time, in He's Bla-ack!

CLEVELAND

Guess who's coming back? Big clue: he's had more than his fair share of bathing mishaps. An even bigger clue: the header above. There's a little look at brand new episode, He's Bla-ack!, On page 72. And we say a proper hello – and whatnot – to Cleveland Brown, on page 73. There, we also remind ourselves exactly what has been going on in that house since Cleveland left for Stoolbend. Let's just say that Peter's been keeping his toilet seat warm for him. That's what friends are for…

Cleveland may have missed out on a few road trips with the guys, but he more than makes up for it in season 12, with a heavenly quest, in 3 Acts of God (page 75).

It's good to have him back. Here's a tip for this season: stick to quick showers. Downstairs, if possible.

Loretta:
"I cheat on you and you apologise to me? Cleveland Brown, you are pathetic!"

Cleveland:
"I disagree, but I respect your candour."

(The Cleveland-Loretta Quagmire)

THE PEWTERSCHMIDTS

"Lois Griffin: daughter of shipping industrialist, Carter Pewterschmidt and passive-aggressivist, Barbara Pewterschmidt."
(Running Mates)

Mr and Mrs Moneybags…
Carter and Barbara live quite the life. They may be rich beyond anybody's wildest dreams, but are they happy, eh? Probably.

In Season 12, when Carter's not trying to ruin Christmas for everybody, in Christmas Guy (page 61), he's regressing to his teen years with Chris (and leaving him everything in his will). Barbara, meanwhile, takes after her model daughter, Lois, as cover girl for 'Veins Magazine', in Fresh Heir (page 66). There's a treat to look out for!

THE GOLDMANS

Who knew that Mort Goldman used to manage a record label? The brilliantly named "Mort Town", no less… He's taking on the freshly-revealed talents of Peter and Quagmire, in Season 12 episode In Harmony's Way (page 60). We're also delving into the past and looking back at that European adventure, in the classic Road to Germany, on page 24. Mort may no longer remember it, but we do.

And who can forget son Neil's infamous helicopter kiss? Your toes will curl, when you land on page 30, for Meg's Most Mortifying Moments. He's still trying to impress her – this time with his 'disarm a bully' skills – in new episode, A Fistful of Meg (page 57).

Muriel Goldman may be gone, but she's certainly not forgotten. Quahog's fallen citizens are remembered, on page 41.

CHANNEL 5 NEWS

Tom Tucker: One-time Hollywood actor, one-time Meg crush and now all-the-time anchor on Quahog's 5 News (Hollywood's loss, eh?). Tom's bringing Brian some news that may just interest him, in the Season 12 episode Brian's a Bad Father (page 64). And his life-changing broadcasts lead the Griffins on an Italian adventure, in Boopa-dee Bappa-dee (page 58).

Who can forgive co-anchor, Joyce Kinney, for her expose on Lois? Joyce features in Lois' (Not-So) Hidden Talents on page 22. And if you didn't know her real last name, it's in our A to Z of Family Guy on page 18 – where Tricia Takanawa also gets a mention.

Diane Simmons may now be in the great newsroom in the sky, but she also joins Muriel Goldman, in our In Memoriam tribute, on page 41.

Tom: "We go live with the local blind man. Sir, how did you suddenly summon the courage to save your friend from that burning building?"

Peter: "That freaking place was on fire?!"

Tom: "And there you have it. Coming up next...Watch me shave."

(Blind Ambition)

FESTIVE FAMILY GUY

"Merry Christmas to all, and to all shut the hell up."

It's the most wonderful time of the year: magical lights on the tree, shiny gifts given with love, a-wassailing in the snow - the parties! - brand new Annuals in the shops (hi!), that holiday hit on a loop, aaaand…the anticipation of when those family arguments will kick off. Merry Christmas!

This year's is extra-joyous for Stewie - as you can find out all about in our look at new episode, Christmas Guy (on page 61). As Peter is all too aware, the festive season would not be same without a good old Christmas TV special, so, let's make like some kind of Dickensian ghost, and revisit the Griffins' Christmas Past…

A Very Special Family Guy Freakin' Christmas

When Peter, on a festive night out, accidentally gave all the family's presents to Toys for Toddlers, Lois took it well. When Brian went to check on the turkey and a fire started, leaving the living room a gutted, foam-filled, broken-televisioned mess… she was pretty pragmatic about it. But when she subsequently learned that they had run out of paper towels? The rage…And this gem of a rant:

"You all think Christmas just happens, you think all this goodwill just falls from the freakin' sky… Well, it doesn't! It falls out of my holly jolly butt!"

A Hero Sits Next Door

Remember when the Swansons moved in next door, and Joe was the most impressive man who'd ever graced Spooner Street (much to Peter's annoyance)? And remember how he told the story of a Christmas Eve orphanage robbery investigation, and the subsequent snowy-rooftop battle with a fabled, Christmas-hating spoilsport that had cost him the use of his legs?

"You think you have won,
You think all is well,
But kiss my green ass
I shall see you in hell!"

Ho-Ho-Hold up! It was all a big fat lie. Exposed in Joe's Revenge, there was no Christmas hating criminal. There was no orphanage. There was no battle. It was all down to "Bobby 'the Shirt' Briggs" and a top-secret-investigation-gone-wrong - featuring Joe Swanson's mind-blowingly brilliant undercover name: "Joe Swansonson".

Joe: *"I lied because I was ashamed of the real story. That I let a vicious criminal get away."*

Jesus, Mary & Joseph!

Peter loves a spot of storytelling. There was that time, while decorating the tree, that he regaled the family with the "the greatest story ever told…A story that goes back over a hundred years: the story of Christmas and the Immaculate Conception". In case they were in any doubt, he made sure to add: "You guys were born the dirty way."

The Biblical cast of his imagination looked surprisingly familiar – down to the donkey – and the newborn king was a baby genius, with a 'modified' manger, fired up to take down the evil Carter Pewterschm – we mean King Herod.

Stewie [in his starring role, as Baby Jesus]: *"Okay, nobody touch my hair, I'm growing it out. Also, I'm gonna start dieting and working out, so I'm, like, crazy lean for the, y'know, for-for the, for the thing."*

Road to the North Pole

And then there was Stewie and Brian's not-so-secret-Santa mission… Stewie turned against his festive hero and intended to kill him for snubbing him at the mall. But he and Brian soon changed course, and set out on an altogether more altruistic endeavour – even if it ultimately went gruesomely wrong. Their new mission? To save Christmas. (You can read more about this one in Brian and Stewie's Road to Friendship, on page 24.)

The theme of this North Pole special: lessen your yuletide demands and be grateful for what you have. Something the Griffins – and we, too - are reminded of this year, through the heartstring-pinging, Brian-based events…

Stewie: *Oh, interesting, interesting theory, Brian. Um, who else isn't real? Hmm? Y-You gonna tell me Elmo isn't real? Huh? SpongeBob? Is he not real, Brian? Is he-Is SpongeBob not there at the bottom of the ocean giving Squidward the business? Hmm? And what about Curious George? Huh? Does he not really exist? Hmm? Is Curious George not really out there makin' little boats out of newspapers that he should be delivering? Huh? Educate yourself, you fool.* (Road to the North Pole)

SOCIAL STATUS: THE

When Family Guy first started, way back in January 1999, the internet was still very much in its infancy. We'd never heard of music streaming, we'd heard too much already of that dial-up connection tone, and a 'device' was one of Stewie's doom-mongering inventions...

So much has changed in Stewie's short life – and not just his slightly-more-tolerant attitude towards Lois. Now, everyone's glued to their gadgets – and even Peter's au fait with cat pictures... (You'll see he's Quagmire's initial choice of IT support in Season 12 episode, Quagmire's Quagmire).

Social networking has also taken hold. Peter's been known to go by the name of "PumpkinEater69" (see above). And in brand new episode, Boopa-Dee Bappa-Dee, Peter renounces the family's nationality on the "Italian social networking site, 'Shut-up-a-you-facebook'".

But what else are they yammering about online?
Well, let's imagine, shall we...

GRIFFINS ONLINE

STEWIE

#stupiddog

StewieGriffin:
I'm the dog. I'm well-read and have a diverse stock portfolio, but I'm not above eating grass clippings and regurgitating them on the small braided rug near the door.

(From Lethal Weapons)

BrianGriffin:
I'm a pompous little antichrist, who'll probably abandon my plans for world domination when I grow up and fall in love with a rough trick named Jim.

#shutupmeg **BRIANGRIFFIN** likes this (from Meg and Quagmire)

#shutupmeg **CHRISGRIFFIN** likes this (from Meg and Quagmire)

BRIAN

#briansays

BrianGriffin:
If dogs aren't supposed to eat dental floss out of the garbage, why do they make it mint flavoured?"

#crazyweekend

(From: Fast Times at Buddy Cianci Jr. High)

StewieGriffin:
Y'know, despite all the craziness this weekend, I feel like a lot of people were lookin' at me like I was really attractive? Which makes me think that I'm gonna grow up to be really good looking!

BrianGriffin:
What part of that statement is supposed to lure me into a conversation?

StewieGriffin:
I talk to you about wet tennis balls...

BrianGriffin:
Oh come on!

StewieGriffin:
We're in a fight!

(From: And Then There Were Fewer)

STEWIE GRIFFIN ADDED 5 PICTURES TO THE ALBUM: **SHUT UP MEG!**

FRIENDS:

MEG GRIFFIN

CHRISGRIFFIN

Relationship Status: **SINGLE** (VERY SINGLE)

NEILGOLDMAN likes this

MEG

ChrisGriffin:
My dad is smarter than your dad.

PETERGRIFFIN likes this

MegGriffin:
We have the same dad, idiot!

ChrisGriffin:
Yeah, but mine's smarter!

(From: Petarded)

+1 Friend Request

CHRIS

MegGriffin:
Wow, Chris, did you lose weight?

ChrisGriffin:
Uh, maybe. I've been working out!

MegGriffin:
Well, you look wicked skinny - I'm, like, jealous!

ChrisGriffin:
Thanks Meg, I'm jealous of your moustache!

MegGriffin:
I don't have a moustache, do I!?

LoisGriffin:
Oh, honey, it's fine. It makes you look distinguished.

(From: He's Too Sexy for His Fat)

Relationship Status: **MARRIED** TO LOIS GRIFFIN

Works at: **THE PAWTUCKET BREWERY**

PETER GRIFFIN JUST CHECKED IN AT: **THE DRUNKEN CLAM**

PETER

#grindsmygears

PeterGriffin:
You know what really grinds my gears? People in the 19th Century. Why don't they get with the freakin' programme? It's called an automobile, folks. It's much faster than a horse!

(From: North by North Quahog)

LOIS

LoisGriffin:
I'm going through a phase right now where I'm only attracted to handsome men...

(From: North by North Quahog)

BRIAN GRIFFIN, GLENN QUAGMIRE and 62 others like this

A-Z

A ALEX BORSTEIN

The Voice of Lois Grifffin, Tricia Takanawa, Barbara Pewterschmidt, Loretta Brown and others. She's also a writer and supervising producer on the show.

E EPISODE MILESTONES

In production order, the 100th episode was Stewie Kills Lois, the 150th, Brian & Stewie and the 200th, Yug Ylimaf… Here's to Family Guy's big 2-5-0. There aren't too many episodes to go until we reach that one.

I IDA DAVIS

Formerly known as Daniel "Dan" Quagmire – Glen's incredibly glamorous dad… and one-time fling of Brian's.

J JAMES WOODS REGIONAL HIGH SCHOOL

One of Quahog's finest educational establishments, attended by Meg, Chris, Connie and Neil… and – who could forget – the legendary Lando Griffin (who was really Peter in disguise). Named after Rhode Island native, actor James Woods.

K KEVIN SWANSON

Joe and Bonnie's son, and Meg's big boy-next-door crush from Season 1. He was thought to have died in Iraq, but it turns out he faked his own death. Kevin reappeared on Spooner Street in Thanksgiving

O O'BRIAN

Peter's biological dad Mickey McFinnigan's pet sheep, that looks – and acts – more than a bit like Brian. "Whose leg d'you have to hump to get a pint of Guinness around here?" (Peter's Two Dads)

P PAWTUCKET PATRIOT ALE

Not only does Peter Griffin work in the Shipping Department at the Pawtucket Brewery, but also their best-loved beer is his drink of choice. Handy, that.

Q QUAGGLECHEK

Glenn Quagmire's birth name, as revealed in Tiegs for Two. We can only wonder if he'd have been quite the same smoothie, had he kept his original identity. Giggity.

U UR-PETER

Peter Griffin's caveman ancestor, and inventor of the wheel. He also appeared in Untitled Griffin Family History.

V VIRGINIA

Home of Stoolbend, where Cleveland and son relocated to start their own spin-off show. Peter and friends have visited the state - most notably in The Splendid Source. With Cleveland coming back to Quahog, everybody's saving on gas.

W WALTER MURPHY

One of the two main composers on Family Guy (the other is Ron Jones). His highlights include: the theme song, the Emmy-nominated cinematic score for And Then There Were Fewer, and music for the Emmy-winning song 'You've Got a Lot to See'.

OF FAMILY GUY

B BANNED

Family Guy has been banned in Indonesia, Taiwan, Vietnam, Iran, South Korea, South Africa, South America and Malaysa. The Venezuelan Justice Minister even stated that any cable stations which refuse to cease airings of the show would be fined.

CHERRY CHEVAPRAVATDUMRONG

Writer and co-executive producer on the show. Peter rearranges the letters in her name to say "Chemotherapy vanguard vCr", in the opening credits of Jesus, Mary & Joseph. Her surname also appears as the real last name of Channel 5 news anchor, Joyce Kinney.

THE DRUNKEN CLAM

Peter's favourite bar, and second home, since (at least) 1977. It survived a British invasion (in One if by Clam, Two if by Sea) and used to be owned by Horace. After his death (in Save the Clam), Jerome stepped in to rescue the place for the guys.

FRANZ GUTENTAG

Puppeteer and former Nazi. Real name: Franz Schlechtnacht. He befriends Chris in German Guy, is recognised by Herbert as his old adversary from World War II, and doesn't make it out of the episode alive…

GENIE

If "boneless Peter" is one of your favourite images of all time, you have this fella to thank, in Family Guy Viewer Mail #1.

H HERBERT

That voice! That whistle! That zimmer frame! That, er, unhealthy obsession with teenage boys…

That's all we're saying.

LARRY AND STEVE

Seth Macfarlane's animated short films, Life of Larry and Larry & Steve - which originated at Rhode Island School of Design - led to the development of Family Guy as we know it.

MILES "CHATTERBOX" MUSKET

Quahog's founding father first featured in Fifteen Minutes of Shame. You can hear more about the man, the legend, in brand new Season 12 episode, Finders Keepers.

NEIL GOLDMAN

Mort's Meg-loving son is named after one half of the writing team Neil Goldman and Garrett Donovan. Their Family Guy episodes include Mind Over Murder, Da Boom and Running Mates.

REDHEAD

Everybody's favourite redhead, Lois was originally blonde in the Family Guy pitch pilot. Who knew? Now you do.

S SETH MACFARLANE

Without him, you would never have heard of Family Guy, and you'd be reading some other Annual right now, instead. Did you know there's a street named after him, one block from the Griffins' house? It's called "McFar Lane", funnily enough

TOWEL BOY

Peter attended to the Pewterschmidts' drying needs (and fell in love with wet-look Lois) through his job at the fancy Newport Country Club. His in-laws will never let their "son-in-lard" forget his lowly past (or present).

XYLOPHONE

As is traditional in A to Zs, X is very much for Xylophone. They're a staple instrument of Family Guy's musical numbers – see Stewie and Brian's unconventional percussive interlude in 'Bag of Weed' (Episode 420).

YODELER

Remember the cutaway where the Griffins take a vacation with the "Price is Right yodeler"? Yes? Good. No? See It Takes a Village Idiot, and I Married One.

ZOMBIES!

Also from It Takes a Village Idiot, and I Married One: Peter brings home a reanimated corpse. And in other Zombie news, Mayor West is terrified of them, believing the undead to be oh-so real - and ordering all graves to be covered with cement.

PETER GRIFFIN'S School Days

In Season 12, episode 3, Acts of God, Peter goes to college, to learn to count to three. He also takes the opportunity to educate himself in The Most Interesting Man in the World.

So, let's look back right now at his academic life how it was and how it might have been, had he been blessed with a few more brain cells (and had he focused his considerable energies on learning).

Most spirited

Most likely to be president

Class Clown

Most athletic

If you search for Peter Griffin's yearbook picture online (go on, we dare you!), you may see a similar looking fella. This face here, though, is 100% official!
PETER:
"Look at this, Lois. See? Right here. I was voted most likely to succeed."
LOIS:
"Peter, that's not you. That's not even a yearbook. That's a People magazine."
PETER:
"I wondered why they had the wrong picture and name."
(A Picture is Worth 1,000 Bucks)
FG
12345
MR
M-
M+
MU
+/-
7
8
4
5
9
1

Lois' (Not-So) Hidden Talents

She's been a lounge singer (in Mind Over Murder), a model (in Model Misbehaviour), an adult movie star (revealed in And I'm Joyce Kinney) and a side show attraction ("me likey bouncy!" – as seen in Lethal Weapons). Yes, there's more to Lois than the wife and mother she's so often taken for granted as. But we're not just talking about her raunchy side.

Lois majored in journalism and successfully auditioned as a news reporter (in FOX-y Lady) – and she's also revealed exceptional sporting prowess. Not only was she selected for the Summer Games diving team (thwarted by her pregnancy with Meg – as shared in Stewie Griffin: The Untold Story), but she's also been a hit in the boxing ring, a smash in the dojo, and a big ol' triumph in the bowling alley, as we're about to find out...

Total Recall

When Peter gets sick, and his voice goes all deep, Lois is turned on. It's like she has a "secret lover"... So Peter's not at all happy when he recovers. He's determined to get the ill-guy magic back, but unfortunately, this time, he becomes dangerously sick, and must forfeit his place at a bowling tournament. Lucky then, that Lois is a total bowling-lane legend! Teammates Quagmire and Joe, or "Quags and Swanny", as she likes to call them, quickly accept her as one of the guys, and they win the trophy. Why, of course!

Lethal Weapons

When Lois tries out Taejitsu with Bonnie, she quickly ascends the ranks to become her teacher's star pupil. And, after Peter patronises her, she agrees to accept an invitation into the advanced class. There's no messing with Lois, so Peter uses her skills to his advantage, to successfully take on the annoying out-of-towners – "the leafers" – who've descended on Quahog to admire the colourful fall foliage. At her black-belt graduation ceremony, Lois challenges the sensei to a fight, breaking "the spiritual bond of the student-master relationship". To paraphrase Stewie, victory is hers!"

"She floats like a butterfly and stings like when I pee!"

Baby You Knock Me Out

It's true: Lois is a knockout and Peter is punching well above his weight (all 293 pounds of it). We know this. So when Quagmire buys Peter tickets to "Foxy Boxing" for his birthday, and Peter puts forward his missus, the sparks fly, in the ring and at home. Lois is a brilliant fighter, who quickly rises the ranks, to become known as "Quahog's Greatest Fighter" and the "Ovarian Barbarian". Lois is ready to throw in the towel, but when the intimidating fighting machine that is Deidre "Action" Jackson challenges her to a match (by 'milking' Peter's boobs in public...) the gloves are off – and Lois wins!

Brian and Stewie's
ROAD TO...FRIENDSHIP

You can discover a lot about a person by travelling with them – and not just their wildly irritating habits. So, how better to understand Brian and Stewie's often antagonistic but ultimately beautiful relationship, than by looking back at their 'Road to' adventures...

ROAD TO RHODE ISLAND - *Season 2*

Brian's drinking is way out of control, and his therapist believes he needs to confront his mother about abandonment issues. Handy then, that when Stewie needs picking up from the Pewterschmidts' place in Palm Springs, it all goes horribly wrong. They lose their tickets home, are forced to do a runner from a terrifying motel, and their plan to procure a private plane is scuppered by lack of any actual flying ability. While sneaking a ride on the back of a truck, Brian sees a sign for Austin, Texas, and leads Stewie to the farm where he was born. Brian's reunited with his mother, Biscuit, but not quite in the way he'd hoped...

FRIENDSHIP DEFINING MOMENT...

Stewie's attempted eulogy at Brian's mother's funeral. *"I never knew Biscuit as a dog, but I did know her as a table. She was sturdy, all four legs the same length..."*

STEWIE

"Oh here's a pleasant sight: Cirrhosis the Wonder Dog."

MUSICAL NUMBER...

Road to Rhode Island

ROAD TO EUROPE - *Season 3*

For such a sharp mind, Stewie's television-viewing choices can be a tad surprising, but he's ultimately a baby, and made-up Brit show Jolly Farm Revue satisfies all of his childish needs. Hooked, and desperate to meet star "Mother Maggie", Stewie sneaks onto a plane and Brian follows. But that plane isn't heading to the UK at all. Whoops! Cue a Middle Eastern adventure, a papal hot air balloon trip and a train ride through the heart of Europe – all leading Stewie to the very definition of disappointment...

FRIENDSHIP DEFINING MOMENT...

Brian's successful attempt to make Stewie feel better about '"fake" *Jolly Farm: "You wanna take a dump in Mother Maggie's shoes? Okay, let's go take a dump in Mother Maggie's shoes."*

STEWIE

"Home? I have no intention of returning to that disgusting hovel, with that intolerable woman, that fat slob and that insufferable dog. Oh, you're right here, aren't you? Oh well, I stand by it."

MUSICAL NUMBER...

You and I are so Awfully Different

ROAD TO RUPERT - *Season 5*

Stewie is devastated when Brian accidently sells his teddy bear, Rupert, at a yard sale, but tracks down the new owner using DNA from the dollar bill used to make the payment. According to the federal database, Rupert's new family live just down the road, but when they arrive the house is empty and a removal truck is leaving. Stewie and Brian "follow that truck!" - which hits a road bump. A box flies out, revealing Rupert's new address. They hitchhike across the country and Stewie performs a musical number in payment for a helicopter to Aspen. They crash, but finally make it to Rupert's new home, where Stewie challenges his possessive new owner to a "ski off"...

MUSICAL NUMBER...

The Worry Song

FRIENDSHIP DEFINING MOMENT...

Stewie makes a speech about finally growing up and moving on, but Brian knows how he really feels: *Stewie: "You're not really gonna live with them are you?" Brian: "No. You're not really over Rupert, are you?" Stewie: "No."*

ROAD TO GERMANY - *Season 7*

It's party time at the Griffins and Mort Goldman is desperate to poop. Sadly Meg's in the bathroom, but – sweet relief! – he stumbles upon a "porta-potty". Unfortunately, it's actually Stewie's time machine, and Mort ends up in 1939 Poland. Brian and Stewie track him down at his grandpa's wedding – just as the Nazis invade. With Stewie's return pad not working, their only option is to flee occupied Poland and somehow make it to England. Which they do – with a now incredibly cranky Mort – via motorbike and U-boat. Stewie needs uranium to fix the time machine, so he infiltrates the Royal Air Force, and, with his Quahog companions, heads to Berlin, where they bump into a terrifying figure from history...

FRIENDSHIP DEFINING MOMENT...

The bonds of Brian and Stewie's friendship are strengthened through physically demanding teamwork... carrying the complaining, petulant Mort to safety.

STEWIE *[to Brian]:*

"What are you doin' in my room? Don't touch my stuff with your dirty, 'walking on the street' paws.""

MUSICAL NUMBER...

Mort the Jew

ROAD TO THE MULTIVERSE - *Season 8*

At the Quahog Clam Day Fair, Stewie introduces Brian to a strange, muscular, genetically perfect pig, and shows him a remote control that enables them to travel the Multiverse. The pig is from an alternate universe, one thousand years more advanced. The theory of the Multiverse is that "every possible eventuality exists", so the two of them set out to explore as many as they can - including a universe where "everyone has to take a poop right now", one where "everyone has two heads" and the "universe of misleading portraiture". All is good, and Brian's enjoying the "universe where dog and human roles are reversed", when he accidentally breaks Stewie's remote and they are stuck. Luckily, they're about to run into some familiar characters...

FRIENDSHIP DEFINING MOMENT...

Brian is forced to pick up Stewie's poop, in the universe run by dogs:
Stewie: "Go on, pick it up, do it, pick up my poop!" Brian: "I need a plastic bag." Stewie: "Here's a thin napkin."

MUSICAL NUMBER...

It's a Wonderful Day for Pie!

ROAD TO THE NORTH POLE - *Season 9*

Stewie is desperate to see Santa at the mall, but by the time they reach the front of the queue, Santa packs up for the day. Stewie, upset, convinces Brian to drive him to the North Pole – or so he thinks. Brian tries to fool him with "Santa's Village", in Rhode Island, instead. There, angry Stewie reveals his plan to kill Santa for blowing them off. He's determined to make it to the actual North Pole, and hitches a ride in a truck, but causes an epic crash. With the help of a friendly Canadian, the Northern Lights and an enchanted totem, they eventually find their way. They are finally face-to-face with Mr Claus, but he's not what Stewie expects. Increasing present demands have turned Christmas into a horror show, featuring mutant elves, wild, feral reindeers and a very sick Santa. So, Brian and Stewie set out to save the day...

FRIENDSHIP DEFINING MOMENT...

Although their relationship reaches some, er, 'frosty' points in this one, it is Brian's instinct to protect Stewie that ultimately drives their journey to the North Pole.

STEWIE

"I am so excited to see Santa Claus! You know what I think is really wonderful? Of all the malls in this great country of ours, he chooses to come here, year after year, y'know? I-I mean. Who are we?! Y'know? I'll tell you who we are. The lucky ones!"

MUSICAL NUMBER...

All I Really want for Christmas,
Christmastime is Killing Us

ROADS TO VEGAS - *Season 11*

When Brian wins tickets to Vegas, Stewie suggests using his recently completed Teleportation Device, to save on travel time. Nothing happens, so they get a plane instead. But, unbeknownst to them, a duplicate version of them has been teleported, whose luck is very much in. The air-travelling original duo miss out on every opportunity that their quicker, charmed clones scoop up, and they end up down and out and in danger. But it isn't long before both pairs face serious jeopardy in Sin City...

FRIENDSHIP DEFINING MOMENT...

Brian and Stewie face the reality of life without each other. Although, technically, they did just cause each other's demise...

[Stewie and Brian standing on hotel balcony railings]

BRIAN AND STEWIE *"1... 2... 3!"*

[Brian jumps; Stewie doesn't]

STEWIE

"I'm sorry I can't, I want to live! I didn't really think we were going to do it!"

BRIAN *[falling]: "You dick!"*

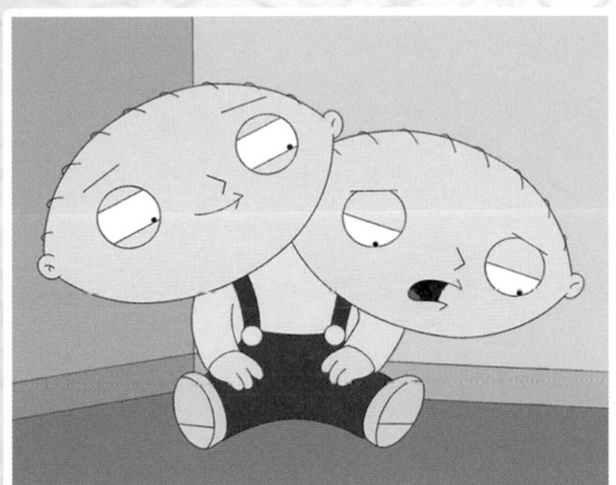

U.S.A

ROCKY ROAD TO...RHODE ISLAND BARS

LONG JOURNEYS, LOW BLOOD SUGAR, SHORT TEMPER...FEELING CRANKY? WE'VE ALL BEEN THERE. HERE'S A QUICK AND EASY CHOCOLATE-BASED TREAT. MAYBE SLIP SOME INTO STEWIE'S BACKPACK, YEAH? CRISIS OVER!

INGREDIENTS

- 6 tbsp of golden syrup
- 250g of soft butter
- 600g of chocolate, broken into pieces (dark, milk, or a mix of dark and milk chocolate)
- 300g of digestives, ginger biscuits or graham crackers
- 150g of marshmallows (mini, or chopped up very small)
- 150g mix of sultanas, raisins, chopped up dried apricots, glace cherries, honeycomb candy, coarsely chopped toasted nuts (like almonds), etc (take your pick!)
- 1 pinch of icing sugar, to dust

METHOD

- Heat the chocolate, butter and syrup in a heavy-based saucepan over a low heat.
- Take the pan off the heat, remove about a quarter of the mixture and keep this for the topping.
- Crush up the biscuits/graham crackers (in a plastic bag with a rolling pin) until some are crumbs but there are still pieces left.

Mix the biscuits, marshmellows and your other ingredients (except the icing sugar) into the larger quantity of chocolate mixture.

- Tip the mixture into a 20cm x 30cm baking tin and smooth the top.
- Pour the chocolate mixture you have saved for the topping over the top and spread out.
- Put in the fridge for about two hours or overnight.
- To serve, cut into 48 pieces and dust with icing sugar.

20 mins prep – and no baking required!

FLOOR IT!
WE'RE SO NAUGHTY

BRIAN AND STEWIE

Wish you were here...

Royally pissed

GETTING STONED IN

GREECE

What the Zeus!

OLE!
Sexy Senorita

FLAMENGO
GABALES

VENI, VIDI, VENICE • VENI, VIDI, VENICE

MEG'S MOST MORTIFYING MOMENTS

Growing up is hard to do. Kids can be so cruel. And so can Meg's own family. In Season 12, we're finding that even her first name is actually a Peter prank. Ahh, "Megatron" Griffin...Check her birth certificate if you don't believe us. He even stole her cutaway gag, once. When she's not being pelted with balls (or meat), or discovering – the hard way – that her butt is the exit to the spirit world, there's romance to contend with. And by 'romance', we don't mean 'having a kidney harvested by your Valentine' – although Meg can tick that one off the list, too. So what do we mean? Time now to hide under a collective duvet of shame, cringe ~~a bit~~ a lot, then remember it's not about you. It's about Meg. And her Most Mortifying Moments...

HER FIRST KISS

Neil Goldman likes Meg. He really likes her. If only

she liked him back. When they both landed internships with Channel 5 News, and ended up facing certain death in a helicopter, at the hands of a killer, the eyes of the world were upon them (or at least the eyes of Quahog). Meg realised she had never been kissed, and guess who was happy to oblige? Yep, Smoothie Goldman. All she had to do was imagine his face was her mega-crush Tom Tucker's, instead – where was the harm? On TV, that's where. A swift rescue followed, and lifelong mortification. If only that were where her embarrassment ended...

HER FIRST, ER, 'MORE THAN A KISS'

In Don't Make Me Over, Meg got glamorous. Goodbye hat, hello highlights... Her talents didn't end there, though, she was about to become a singing sensation. Meg Griffin caught the eye of a certain prime time Saturday night TV host, they became, er, 'amorous', and then... the big revelation that the whole thing was the show's opening sketch, and Meg had been used for comedy. It's probably on the internet forever, now. If only the cringe stopped there...

IS EVERYTHING ON TV?

In Fifteen Minutes of Shame, Meg's humiliation at the hands of her family came to a head in the studio of the talk show, 'Diane'. There, a producer spotted the Griffins' potential, and a reality show was born. That was not the worst of it, though. Soon, Meg was replaced with a 'hot' actress. Not everything was quite so public, though...

IN THE CLOSET

No. It's not all on TV. (Well, apart from us watching, of course.) Sometimes, it's been behind closed doors. And then those doors have opened all-too rudely, to a baying crowd and a mentally scarring revelation.

Like at Connie's Sweet Sixteen, in And the Weiner Is...

It could have been so beautiful. 'Seven minutes in Heaven' with the eminently dateable Doug. What a shame that when those seven minutes were over and the closet doors were opened, dateable Doug's mouth was not the mouth on Meg's. No. That mouth was the mouth of a pig. And cue squealing (from the pig).

Or at Connie's costume celebrations, in Halloween on Spooner Street...

It could have been so beautiful... 'Seven minutes in Heaven' with mystery big guy, 'Optimus Prime'... What a shame that when those seven minutes were over and the closet doors were opened, that mystery man turned out to be... her very own brother, Chris. Making out with his now unmasked sibling, Meg. And cue the horror...

MEG: "Oh my God! We did so much!"

Two tips: Avoid Connie. Avoid closets.

OUT OF THE CLOSET

Her own mother kissing her 'girlfriend'...

Remember Meg's lab partner, Sarah, in Brian Sings and Swings? Meg was thrilled to make a new friend at school and finally be accepted into a club, even if it meant she had to pretend to be gay. How embarrassing when her own mother confronted her about her true sexuality, and proved her point by showing Meg how to kiss a woman.

And while we're talking about Lois...

Her own mother kissing her 'boyfriend'...
It wasn't enough that Meg finally met a seemingly decent guy to be with. In Go, Stewie, Go, the whole of Quahog, Channel 5 News, God and the Giant Chicken descended on the Griffin household to have a look-see. Oh, and Cleveland made a 500-mile trip from Stoolbend to very briefly witness this momentous occasion.

Why, then, did Lois have to spoil it, by making a move? And why did this supposedly incredible fella make out with Meg's mother? Life is so unfair!

INTENSE INFATUATIONS

Unrequited obsessions are Meg's speciality – and they're not always so Tom-Tucker innocent. There's an unnerving dark side to Meg, that we glimpse more often than is comfortable, and which probably isn't helped by the way her family treat her. Who could forget when Meg took care of Joe for Bonnie, in The Hand That Rocks the Wheelchair? Or the whole Brian thing?

How about watching cartoons in bed with Mayor West? That's not embarrassing at all. We'll tell you what is though. This:

We could go on. Probably best to draw a line right here. This cringe-fest could fill a book of its own. Oh yeah... Meg's diary. Provider of much amusement to the Griffin family since 1999.

LOIS: "Honey, give me any laundry you have. I'm doing a diapers and Meg load."

(Friends Without Benefits)

THE WIT AND WISDOM OF CHRIS GRIFFIN

Kids say the darndest things...particularly if they're called Chris Griffin...

"Wow, a parade! It's like I'm walking past stuff, but I'm not going anywhere!"
(Roads to Vegas)

Chris: "I don't want to get rid of my zit, I like him. He's my friend. His name is Doug."
Brian: "I just wish I didn't have to look at it."
Chris: "Well, we have to look at your ANUS all day!"
Stewie: "Thank you."
(Brian the Bachelor)

Chris: "Brown is the color of poo. Ahahahahaha!"
Brian: "Yes, yes it is."
(The Story on Page One)

Chris: "You're a dog! You don't have a soul!"
Brian: "Oww."
(North by North Quahog)

"I just want peace on Earth. That's better than being selfish like Meg, right?
So I should get more than her."
(A Very Special Family Guy Freakin' Christmas)

"My name is Chris, I'm supposed to be on my best behaviour tonight and not mention poo...Oh, God! What have I done?!"
(The Kiss Seen Around the World)

Chris: "Hey Dad, why don't you invent the frisbee, that's an awesome toy."
Meg: "It's already been invented."
Chris: "Then how come I never heard of it?"
(The King is Dead)

"They have this game where you put in a dollar and you win four quarters. I win every time!"
(Chitty Chitty Death Bang)

"I'm not fat, I'm Rubenesque!"
(Emission Impossible)

Lois: "Is she nice?"
Chris: "Yeah, she's really nice and super-pretty and her bicycle seat smells like strawberries."

Lois: "Oh, Okay..."
Chris: "I'm going to go upstairs and alternate between hopeful excitement and suicidal pessimism."
(Tom Tucker: The Man and his Dreams)

Chris [to Meg]: Excuse me, I was wondering if you would go to the dance with me on Friday?
Meg: "Chris, it's me. Meg."
Chris: "Ah, well. That's everybody."
(Leggo my Meg-O)

Peter: "It's good to have you back, buddy."
Chris: "Thanks dad – I didn't really fit in there anyway. The rooms were only 15 by 20. Ahhahahahahahahh! If I didn't learn to laugh at myself, I'd be dead right now."
(No Chris Left Behind)

Chris [on movies]: "The eagle was majestic and beautiful, but sometimes you have to sacrifice spectacle for a coherent storyline."
(Baby Not on Board)

FAMILY GUY *IN* NUMBERS

"When I stick this army guy with the sharp bayonet up my nose, it tickles my brain. Haha... Ow! Oh, now I don't know math."

(The Kiss Seen Around the World)

CHANNEL 5 NEWS
Channel 5 News was originally *Channel 6 News* in the Family Guy pitch pilot.

00093
The Spooner Street zip code, as revealed in FOX-y Lady.

555-0143 Quagmire's phone number. The evidence is on his left butt cheek, in The Cleveland-Loretta Quagmire.

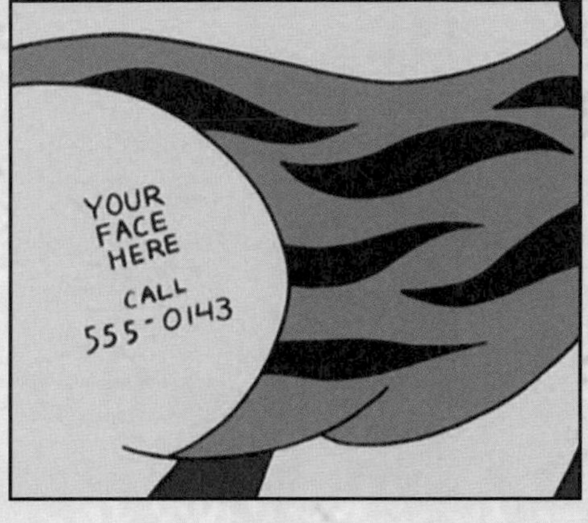

31 The Griffins' house number. Neighbour Quagmire lives at **29** Spooner Street, with the Swansons the other side, at number **33.**

293 Peter's weight in pounds ("since grade school"), which we find out in brand new episode, Vestigial Peter.

11.34am
Stewie's time of birth, shown in Yug Ylimaf.

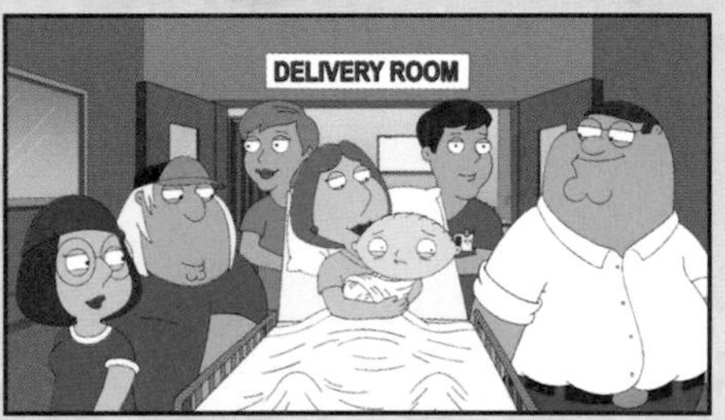

1999 The year Family Guy first aired.

3 "E!"
31 "This!"
0 "Spooky ghost mouth!"
8 "Snowman!"
44 "Two sailboats!"
17 "17!"

The Griffins winning lottery numbers, drawn and announced by "a checkout girl in a cheap dress who wants to be a model", in Lottery Fever.

61 Quagmire's age in FOX-y Lady. (And, according to his driver's licence, he was born in 1948). The secret to his youth? Carrots, apparently.

18 The number of medals Joe has for heroism, as revealed in Blind Ambition.

43 Lois' (crisis) age in Lois Comes out of her Shell.

3 hours 27 minutes
the amount of time it took Brian to write **'Wish It, Want It, Do It'.** "One big steaming pile of book."
(Brian Writes a Bestseller)

2 The number of times Family Guy has been cancelled.

THE COOLEST CAMEOS IN FAMILY GUY

CULT ICONS, A-LIST SUPERSTARS AND ALL-OUT LEGENDS HAVE MADE THE JOURNEY TO QUAHOG. HERE'S A SECTION OF SOME OF THE FINEST GUEST APPEARENCES IN THE HISTORY OF THE SHOW.

CATE BLANCHETT stars as wicked baby Penelope in Mr. & Mrs. Stewie - and Queen Elizabeth II in *Family Guy Viewer Mail No. 2.*

DAVID LYNCH is The Broken Stool's bartender, Gus, in *The Cleveland Show* – who also pops up in *The Splendid Source.*

CARRIE FISHER is Peter's boss Angela at the Pawtucket Brewery.

DEBBIE REYNOLDS (Carrie Fisher's actress mother) stars as Mrs. Wilson in *Tales of a Third Grade Nothing.*

HUGH LAURIE educates Peter in the ways of cricket in *One if by Clam, Two if by Sea,* and he also reprises his TV role as Dr. House in *Business Guy.*

ELLEN PAGE is Chris' Lois-lookalike girlfriend, Lindsey, in *Tom Tucker: The Man and His Dream.*

BEN STILLER appears as himself in *No Meals on Wheels.*

JON HAMM 'dons' the dapper suit, as himself, in *Ratings Guy.*

CHARLIE SHEEN appears as himself in Brian *Griffin's House of Payne.*

DREW BARRYMORE seduces Chris, in *Fast Times at Buddy Cianci Jr. High*, and is also known as Jillian Russell – Brian's not-so-smart girlfriend.

ELIJAH WOOD auditions for the lead in Brian's TV show in *Brian Griffin's House of Payne.*

ALAN BENNETT is not impressed with 'A Passing Fancy', in *Brian's Play.*

CARLY SIMON stars as herself in *Total Recall.*

JAMES WOODS makes many appearances in the show - AND he gets a high school named after him.

DAN ACKROYD & CHEVY CHASE come to stay at Cleveland's old house, in *Spies Reminiscent of Us.*

FRANK SINATRA, JR. brings a touch of class to the proceedings in *Brian Sings and Swings* and *Tales of a Third Grade Nothing.*

JASON SEGEL plays himself, and his role as Marshall Eriksen, in *Peter's Progress.*

RAY LIOTTA is Zack in *Brian Does Hollywood.*

RYAN REYNOLDS becomes obsessed with Peter in *Stewie Goes for a Drive*. He also appears in *Jesus, Mary & Joseph.*

TOM HIDDLESTON voices the statue of Peter's ancestor in *No Country Club for Old Men.*

SEAN BEAN voices the painting of Peter's ancestor in *No Country Club for Old Men.*

IOAN GRUFFUDD'S roles have included Prince Charles in *Family Guy Viewer Mail No. 2.*

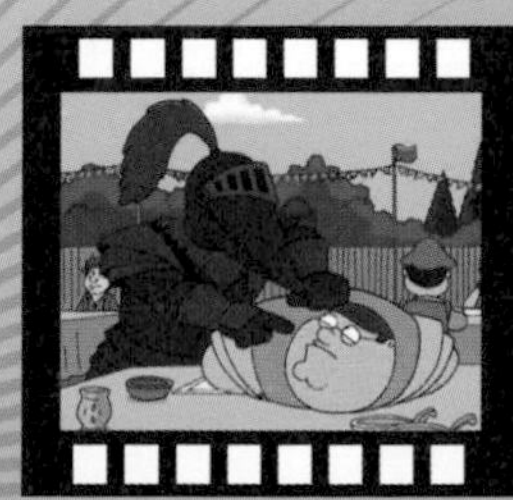

WILL FERRELL is the voice of 'Fat Greek Guy' and Miles 'Chatterbox' Musket, in *Fifteen Minutes of Shame.* He's also The Black Knight, in *Mr. Saturday Knight.*

PATRICK STEWART makes many appearances, including the brilliant internal monologues of baby Susie Swanson.

'YOUR' FAMILY GUY PORTRAIT

LOIS, PETER, MEG OR CHRIS? YOU CAN FIND OUT FOR SURE WHICH GRIFFN YOU ARE WITH OUR PERSONALITY QUIZ, ON PAGE 38. OR, JUST GET SOME PHOTOS OF YOUR FRIENDS' AND FAMILY'S FACES RIGHT THIS MINUTE, TRY 'EM ALL OUT FOR SIZE AND CREATE YOUR OWN FETCHING GROUP SHOT.

"Sorry kids, daddy loves you but daddy also loves TV, and in all fairness TV came first..."

"Butt Scrat

CUTAWAY!

IF, LIKE PETER, YOU'RE NOT MATURE ENOUGH TO USE GROWN-UP SCISSORS, MAKE SURE YOU GET SOME HELP. WE ALL REMEMBER THE TIME HE MADE THAT MASK IN ROADS TO VEGAS...

"SCISSORS ARE JERKS!"

FRAME IT, HANG IT ON YOUR WALL AND SMILE WITH PURE PRIDE, WHY DON'T CHA?

MAKE YOUR OWN...

"Butt Scratcher!"

"Butt Scratcher!"

If the Griffns are ever short on cash, Peter has a very, er, 'handy' sideline...We saw it in No Chris Left Behind, when he attempts to bring in the extra dollars to pay for his big son's education at the swanky Morningwood Academy. You can save yourself the dough though, with this, your very own butt scratcher. You're welcome.

Comedy callback fans, listen out for the "butt scratcher!" sales pitch, during the Lois Griffin vs. Deidre Jackson boxing match, in Baby You Knock Me Out. And, if you're still keen for more, have a little look at (and listen to) a deleted scene from Episode 420...

"Butt Scratcher!"

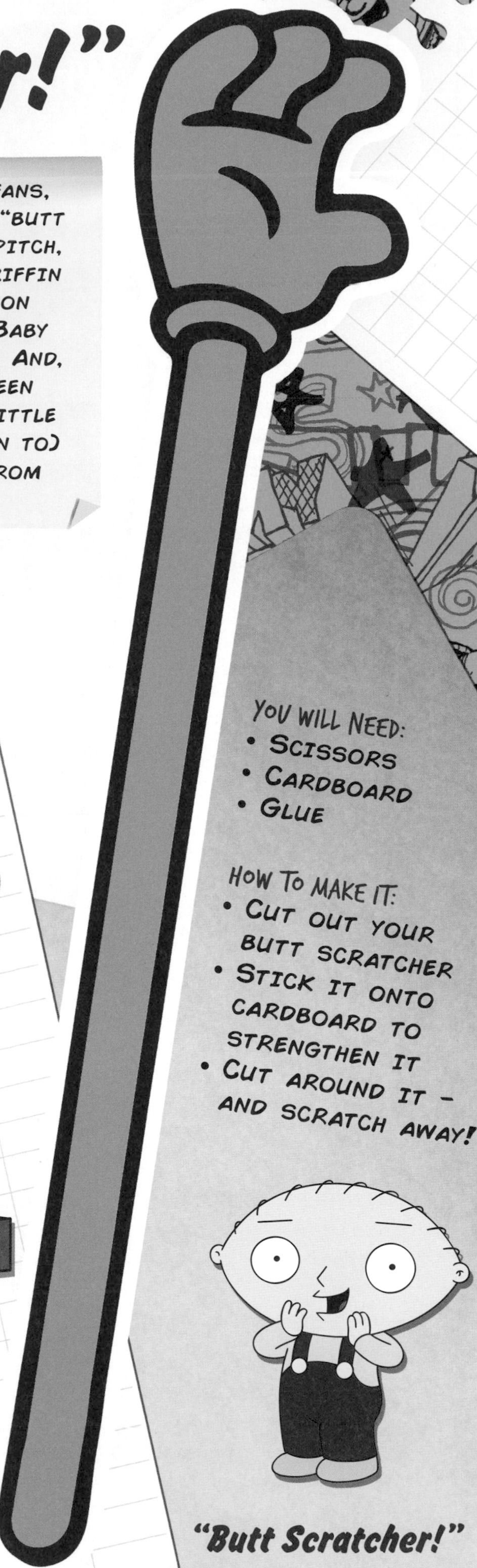

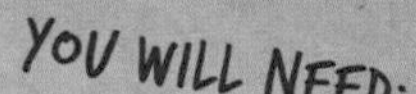

You will need:

- Scissors
- Cardboard
- Glue

How to make it:

- Cut out your butt scratcher
- Stick it onto cardboard to strengthen it
- Cut around it – and scratch away!

"Butt Scratcher!"

Which Griffin are You?

QUIZ!

1) At the tattoo parlour you...

a. Have already got one. No need for more.
b. A tattoo? No freakin' way!
c. Get something large, very visible and ultimately regrettable. You were drunk.
d. Opt for a butterfly. It's what everyone else is getting.
e. Have "serenity" inked on your lower back.
f. A tattoo? That would tickle!

2) It's your birthday...

a. Drinks and music are in order - at a seriously classy establishment.
b. There had BETTER be a party. And presents. Or else.
c. It's decided: Beers with the guys.
d. A party, attractive people and 'Seven Minutes in Heaven'. What could possibly go wrong?
e. No fuss, please. Age is just a number.
f. I'll be in my room.

3) It's movie night! What's your pick?

a. Something arty and European. Black and white, and with subtitles, if possible.
b. Near-future dystopian sci-fi. Or a British historical drama. Whatevs.
c. A 1980's classic. Preferably set in a high school.
d. Teen rom-com.
e. A Hollywood epic. Something weepy.
f. Porn.

4) Oh. The electricity's out - but there are candles. Which book...?

a. Something weighty and profound. An examination of what it means to be alive.
b. Something with colourful – and tactile – pictures of cows and sheep and ducks. Or Machiavelli's The Prince.
c. Comics all the way! Or I'd tell a story.
d. A teen magazine. Something that plays on your insecurities.
e. The latest bestselling bodice-ripper.
f. Porn.

5) Animals are cool. If you could be one - which one?

a. A dog. Every time.
b. Something cute. Or sexy.
c. A lion, or a whale, or a peterodactyl...
d. A donkey.
e. A fox.
f. A monkey! But not an evil one...

6) It's good to have a hobby. What's yours?

a. Working on that novel...
b. I'm a master of invention.
c. TV. Beer.
d. Journaling. Obsessing.
e. Playing the piano – I just don't seem to have the time, these days...
f. Drawing.

7) So... What music are you into?

a. The Rat Pack
b. Musicals
c. 1980s
d. Pop – the latest boyband/idol
e. I used to be in a folk duo
f. Rock

8) What's your drink of choice?

a. Martini
b. Milk
c. Beer
d. Diet soda
e. Wine
f. Regular soda

THE RESULTS

Now that you know who you are, cut out your badge and wear with pride!

Mostly A: You are Brian!

Drinker, thinker...Pretentious? Or just waaay deeper than everybody else? You love the finer things in life, but ask yourself this: are you being true to you?

Mostly B: You are Stewie!

A prodigal talent; the king of cutting remarks... you seem to be somewhat confused about who you are, and this can result in some unjustifiably aggressive behaviour. Remember: you're still young. Life gets easier.

Mostly C: You are Peter!

With the wide-eyed wonder of a child, you love an adventure, a prank, a joke. Smart you aren't, but you do have a very big heart – and this gets you out of a lot of trouble. Don't take this for granted.

Mostly D: You are Meg!

In a family of 'personalities', you're the 'normal' one. You just want to be liked, is that too much to ask? It's no wonder you're needy and whiney – but tone it down a bit, yeah?

Mostly E: You are Lois!

You are one tough cookie, with a deviant streak. You love your family and would do anything to protect them - don't mess with you! Watch out, though, that your family doesn't take advantage...

Mostly F: You are Chris!

Awkward is your middle name (even if your birth certificate has you down as 'Cross') and some people write you off as an idiot – but you have (very well) hidden depths...

The Ultimate Episode Crossword

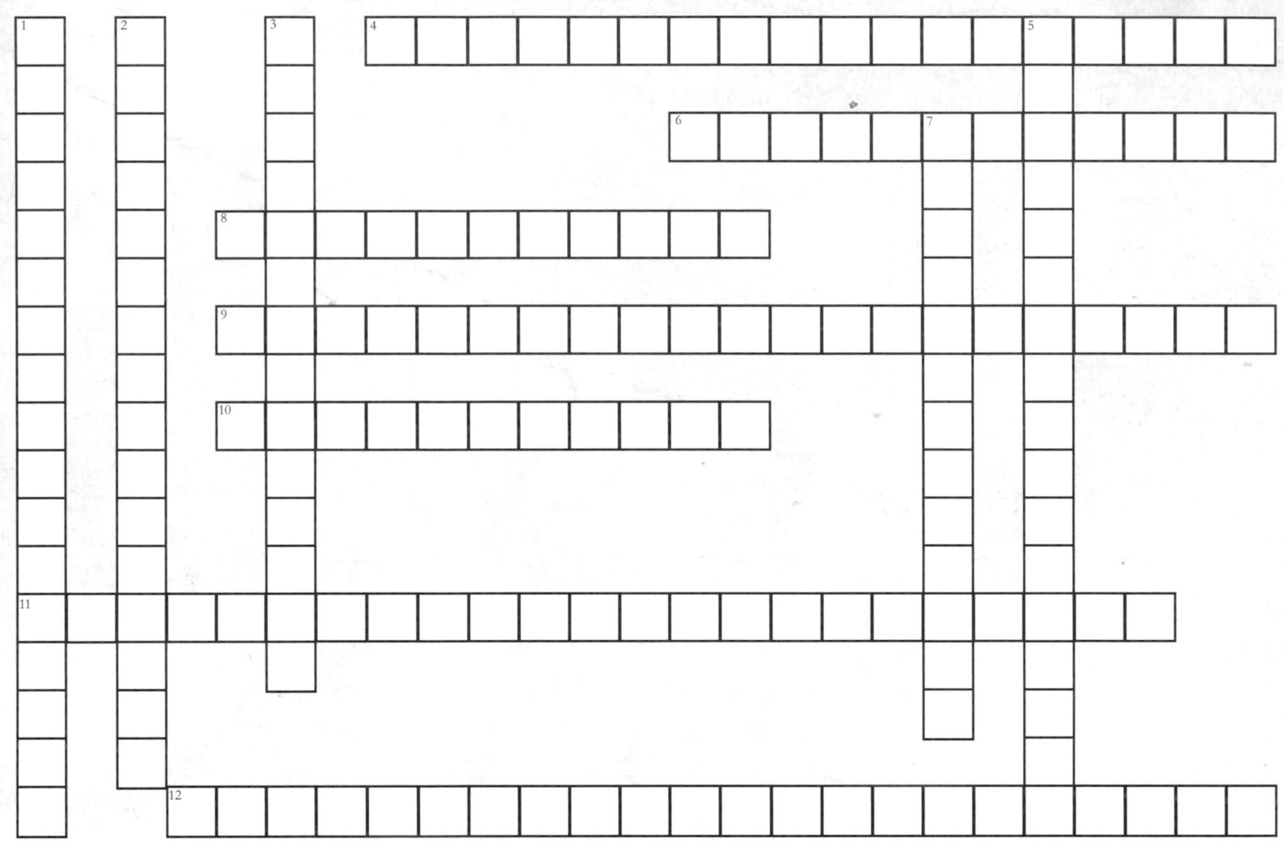

Name that title…

The answers are on page 77.

Across

4. Shipwrecked Peter returns **(3, 7, 8)**
6. When Brian met Ida… **(9, 3)**
8. When Meg interns for Mayor West **(4, 7)**
9. The Griffins inherit a mansion **(5, 5, 6, 5)**
10. Brian takes Meg to the prom **(6, 5)**
11. Peter's panic room story **(3, 7, 6, 7)**
12. Wish It, Want It, Do It **(5, 6, 1, 10)**

Down

1. The Swansons move in **(1, 4, 4, 4, 4)**
2. Stewie discovers his artist ancestor **(3, 3, 4, 6)**
3. Peter discovers he's Mexican **(5, 2, 7)**
5. Peter and the guys on a very funny quest **(3, 8, 6)**
7. "Mass awareness of a certain avian variety…" **(1, 5, 2, 5)**

IN MEMORIAM

It's not all fun times on Family Guy. Sometimes, just sometimes, events take a deadly serious turn. The Griffins are about to face this fact in Season 12. So, as we prepare to say 'farewell' to our favourite clever canine, let's remember the other key Quahog characters who are now dearly (and not-so-dearly) departed.

Muriel Goldman

Our customer-cheating former pharmacy worker met husband Mort through a dating service, sharing a germy first kiss, aged 14. But Muriel met her maker – or, rather, the stabby, murderous Diane - in And Then There Were Fewer. We still miss her, but there's always Mort. If you squint a bit, they could be one and the same.

Diane Simmons

She was responsible for Muriel's death (plus several more), but, in the words of Stewie, her uppance came. Karma is oh-so real…

Tom Tucker's original TV 'other half' (and bitter rival), Diane was an accomplished (albeit often unprofessional) broadcaster, known best for her work on Quahog's Channel 5 News, and as the star of her own television talk show, 'Diane'.

Vain, ambitious and competitive, and so insecure about her looks and future she picked the unthreatening Meg as an intern. Diane turned to murder after her fortieth birthday, in an attempt to frame her co-anchor, who wanted her replaced.

Remember her role as 'The Girl' in black-and-white, 'artistic' clown/pancake student film, Lint (as Diane Seidelman)? Her acting talents really came to the fore in her final episode, And Then There Were Fewer. It took a while to figure out who was the murderer, but when it was finally revealed to be her, Stewie saw to it that she would never perform, kill, or broadcast with Tom Tucker ever again.

Fin.

Loretta Brown

Who could forget Cleveland's first wife? Not Cleveland, in brand new episode Baby Got Black, that's for sure. Particularly as Peter prank calls him – as Loretta herself – to say the death thing has all been a big mistake. Not unlike Loretta's divorce-inducing fling with Quagmire, then.

Loretta was a passionate woman, who channelled this through her acting talents. Her role as Anna in Lois Griffin's production of 'The King and I' was cruelly snatched by Diane Simmons – all thanks to a meddling Peter. And her life was cruelly snatched on The Cleveland Show, in a stunt-turned-bath-gag-gone-wrong. Can you guess who was responsible?

Here's a clue: *Peter Griffin.*

QUIZ! THE FAMILY GUY HIT PARADE

THERE ARE SO MANY SONGS TO CHOOSE FROM, BUT HOW MANY OF THE FOLLOWING DO YOU KNOW?

FILL IN THE BLANKS (AND SING 'EM, IF YOU CAN CARRY A TUNE...).

1. MR. ....

2. DING! .... ARE DONE!

3. THE WORRY ....

4. GOTTA GIVE UP THE ....

5. THIS .... IS FREAKIN' SWEET!

6. .... 4CASH

7. PROM NIGHT DUMPSTER ....

8. A BAG OF ....

9. YOU'VE GOT A LOT TO ....

10. I WANT TO HAVE .... WITH YOU

11. MY DRUNKEN .... DAD

12. IT'S A WONDERFUL DAY FOR ....

13. YOU AND I ARE SO .... DIFFERENT

14. THIS IS ONE FINE DAY TO BE ....

15. PIANO ....

16. .... IS THE BEST THING EVER

17. CAN'T .... ME

18. .... SONGS MEDLEY

19. MY .... BABY

20. YOU ....

'GRIFFIN AND QUAGMIRE'

Peter and Glenn team up to form this dynamic musical duo in the Season 12 episode, In Harmony's Way – which features more songs than any other episode of the show so far! Tunes to tune in for include: 'Credit Card Debt', 'I Can't Poop in Strange Places' and 'Why the Hell Do You Brush Your Teeth at Work?' You can read more about it on page 60.

FIND OUT THE ANSWERS AND THE EPISODES THE SONGS ARE FROM ON PAGE 77.

THE BIG Quahog Quiz!

IT'S TIME TO FIND OUT HOW MUCH YOU REALLY KNOW ABOUT THE SHOW. LET'S GO!

01 What was Tom Tucker's former career?

02 Name the mansion the Griffins inherit from Lois' Aunt Marguerite.

03 Name the country club where Peter and Lois first met.

04 And what was Peter's occupation there?

05 In Fifteen Minutes of Shame, what's the name of the reality show the Griffins star in?

06 When Peter goes undercover at high school, what's his new name?

07 What's the name of James Woods' monkey in 'Brian's' TV show, Class Holes?

08 Who killed Diane Simmons?

09 What's the name of the cartoon that Peter and Chris create in FOX-y Lady?

10 And who are the two main characters in it?

11 What's the name of Peter's falcon, in Call Girl?

12 What is Lois' middle name?

13 What is Quagmire's new - female - name, in Valentine's Day?

14 Who is the boy Meg's obsessed with, in Friends Without Benefits?

15 What's the name of the turtle Stewie finds in Lois Comes Out of Her Shell?

16 Where does Stewie get a job, in Baby Not on Board?

17 What school does Peter attend in Tales of a Third Grade Nothing?

18 What new name does Stewie give to the Quahog Cabana Club, in Tales of a Third Grade Nothing?

19 In No Country Club for Old Men, which instrument does Peter play on a TV talent show?

20 And how is his performance unusual?

21 In the same episode, what's the name of the country club Chris' girlfriend invites the family to?

22 What's the name of Quagmire's purebred Persian cat, featured in Joe's Revenge?

23 Who voices Susie Swanson's inner monologues?

24 What's the name of the dog that the Griffins had before Brian?

....

25 And how old was he when he died?

....

26 What is Lois' sister called?

....

27 And which character did she marry?

....

28 What's Lois' long-lost brother called?

....

29 What was Joe Swanson's undercover name, in Joe's revenge?

....

30 What was Ida Davis' previous name?

....

31 What's the name of Stewie's first teddy bear, who he meets again in Quagmire's Quagmire?

....

32 And who gave him the bear?

....

33 What's the name of Herbert's dog?

....

34 And who voices Herbert's dog?

....

35 What's the full name of Chris' puppeteer friend, in German Guy?

....

36 What's the name of the movie-loving manager of Quahog Mini-Mart'?

....

37 Who voices Tricia Takanawa?

....

38 What's the full name of the most popular girl at James Woods Regional High School?

....

39 What was Peter's mother's name?

....

40 And what was her cat called?

....

41 Which teacher did Drew Barrymore voice?

....

42 Who is Dylan Flannigan?

....

43 What's the name of Stewie's favourite children's TV show, in Road to Europe?

....

44 And in which city is it filmed?

....

45 Who wrote the book Brian keeps in his safety deposit box at the bank, featured in Brian & Stewie?

....

46 What's Tom Tucker's son called?

....

47 And what's Joe Swanson's son called?

....

48 Which year does Peter travel back in time to, in Meet the Quagmires?

....

49 And how does he get there?

....

50 Who is the founding father of Quahog?

....

Quagmire's (Very Random) Acts of Kindness

While his love life is dark, deviant, diseased - and sometimes downright illegal - perhaps surprisingly, it's not always about the "giggity" for Glenn. Sometimes, just sometimes, we'll catch a glimpse of another side to him. Here are a few of those moments...

Unofficial Uncle

"Mr Quagmire" displays his paternal side, in Barely Legal, dishing out the unexpected love-life advice to Meg - albeit in his underwear: This is somewhat undermined, in more recent times, by the incredibly creepy-to-watch "crack onto Meg as soon as she hits 18" plot (in Quagmire and Meg). Oh.

Snuggle Buddy

When Lois decides enough is enough and gets twin beds to avoid being crushed at night by Peter's massive frame, Peter gets lonely. Cue Quagmire, who agrees to offer up his snuggle services, saying: "snuggling is a basic human need". It's a beautiful thing.

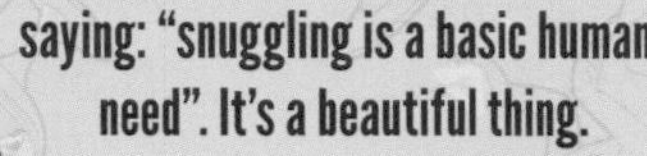

"Well, it's your 18th birthday, Meg. That's a very important milestone in a young girl's...I mean, a young woman's life. Hey, welcome to the adult club, huh? And you know what? You got another member right next door if you ever wanna talk and stuff. Happy birthday. [pats Meg's left leg. His little finger wiggles] Hey...hey, where's that pinkie goin', huh? Where's he goin'? What...what's he doin'? Get back here. There you go. [Meg smiles then looks at Quagmire]"

"Yeah, I date women for their bodies but at least I'm honest about it."

Mr Sensible

There's nothing wrong with baldness, a fact Quagmire tries to accept, when he's caught on camera, his faux hair making a desperate bid for escape. As Peter says: "Wow. I guess all this time Quagmire shoulda been saying 'wiggity'."

Quagmire decides to embrace the natural look – and suddenly loses all of his former personality. It's goodbye 1950's Hawaiian shirts; hello, brown cardigan and slacks. Less "allllrriiiight!" at the ladies; more "slow down!" at passing cars...

But Peter and Joe hate the new, environmentally caring, library-attending Quagmire, and a swiftly performed hair transplant, courtesy of Doctor Hartman, quickly brings him back to his former self. Order: restored.

Cat Man

Let us not forget James, Quagmire's first cat, discovered under his house, in Episode 420. It was a beautiful friendship – and short-lived, thanks to Peter's ill-advised shaving prank. With James, we got a real insight into Glenn's softer side, and it paved the way for Quagmire's next idolised kitty, Principessa – a purebred Persian, no less.
We won't discuss what Brian eventually did to this worshipped cat (in Roads to Vegas). It'll ruin the moment.

"I can trace her lineage to the cats kept by Cleopatra."

Family Guy

We've seen Quagmire taking his sick five-year-old niece Abby to see Santa (in Road to the North Pole); sorting out his sister's violent husband once and for all (in Screams of Silence: The Story of Brenda Q); and realising that the baby daughter, Anna Lee, left on his doorstep (in Quagmire's Baby), has better chances living with her loving adoptive parents. He did initially give her up for adoption because she was messing up his sex life, though.

Mr Romantic

Sometimes Glenn falls hard. And not just for the 1980's love of his life, Cheryl Tiegs (who broke his heart). In I Take Thee Quagmire, Joan the maid turns his world upside down, and shows us this fairytale-version of Glenn again. A whirlwind romance and marriage quickly follow... Until he glimpses Lois' boobs at the wedding reception and remembers himself. Oh dear.

Local Hero

Even Quagmire can't fail to notice he has a perving problem when all of his friends and neighbours confront him for spying on Lois in the bathroom (in Blind Ambition). He's let loose in the mall, after some very unorthodox treatment, and he just can't handle seeing so many women. So he runs away, and ends up in the CCTV room monitoring women's changing rooms (er, "for shoplifters"...). Quagmire thinks he's died and gone to heaven, until he spots a woman having a heart attack and races to her rescue.

After a very 'full-on' resuscitation, a bystander says, "thank god you know CPR!" To which Quagmire replies, "what the hell's CPR?!"

BRIAN: A Dog's Life

It's all too easy to take those you love for granted, and if Brian's your favourite anthropomorphic animal ever, get ready for an emotional rollercoaster in Season 12, as the much-talked-about tragic events play out. But let's not dwell too long on the sad bits. It's time now for the warm glow of nostalgia to descend, as we look back on the life of Stewie's good pal, "Bri".

Family Life

Born near Austin, Texas, eight years ago, to mother Biscuit (who ended up stuffed as a table) and racist father Coco (who was hit by a milk truck), puppy Brian was given up for a better life – and since then, as we know, he's come a pretty long way. Down and out, near Quahog, and whilst washing car windshields, Brian was taken in by the man who was to become his best friend: Peter Griffin.

As Peter says, "he's a member of our family first, and a dog second," but sometimes this family closeness has crossed a big ol' line. Like when Meg developed her terrifying obsession with Brian, in Barely Legal, feeding him her hair in a pie ("part of me is inside of you, Brian. Do you feel me, Brian? Do you feel me inside of you?") - spawning the long-running "Cool Whip" pronunciation gag in the process. Or when Brian 'fessed up to his feelings for Lois, on a trip to Martha's Vineyard. (For the record, Mrs G is not completely immune to his charms...)

As father-for-a-whole-week to teen-son, Dylan, Brian learnt all about the rewards – and worries – of parenting, becoming an insufferable know-it-all as a result:

"You can't hold your kids back. It's like I say: you have to give your kids both roots and wings."

(The Former Life of Brian)

Love Life

If his pursuit of women seems shallow and, er, 'dogged' (sorry), Brian is in fact, deep down, an old romantic at heart. All he really wants is to meet the love of his life – and he knows that this can't be Lois.

His drawn-out relationship with the beautiful (but not-so-smart) Jillian Russell came to an end after their attempt at living together ended badly (not helped by Peter and Stewie). Tracy Flannigan was the "greatest girl" he ever met, and he hoped to rekindle that romance. But time was cruel to Tracy, no longer the woman he remembered (and now mother of his child), and all of a sudden, he was no longer interested. Oh, and then there was Carolyn, the sexy, bookish atheist: the perfect match. What a shame that Brian followed Stewie's "take it slow" advice, without actually communicating his feelings to the woman in question, and she ended up with Cleveland. And then Quagmire.

In an attempt to get to the bottom of Brian's lack of luck with women, Stewie gathers together all of our canine hero's exes, in Valentine's Day in Quahog.
And while Brian may think of himself as sophisticated, intelligent, erudite and well spoken, the consensus amongst his former lovers is that he's "self-absorbed", "pretentious" and "insecure". Or, a "blowhard" with a "tiny penis". Or, in the words of Ida Davis (aka Quagmire's dad): a "wonderful man" – who's "just having a difficult time coming to terms with his sexuality". Don't hold back, ladies.

Literary Life

When Brian's not watching his favourite feminine freshness commercial, singing up a storm with Frank Sinatra Junior, putting on a show on the road with Stewie, drinking, or picking up women, he can often be found workin' on "that novel" (or latest literary endeavour).

Though Brian's efforts so far may be more mediocre than he'd ever realise, it's surely a matter of time before he does in fact come up with the goods. That's the hope he's clinging to. And though Stewie may often be Brian's harshest critic, he's also often his biggest fan - keen to get Brian's opinion on his own play, 'An American Marriage', and spotting his friend's potential:

Brian: *"By the time I'm dead you won't even be ten. You'll have seventy more years to be great. I just wish I coulda had five to be good."*
Stewie: *"There's your voice, Brian. It's a depressing voice, but it's yours. Write from that."* (Brian's Play)

Over the page, we digest his writerly works to date...

Friends for Life

Brian and Stewie... Their friendship was cemented through their many shared adventures - and it's given us some of the biggest laughs and most moving moments in the show. Brian is a sometime surrogate-father figure to Stewie, looking out for him and calling him "kid". And we all know how he handled the diaper situation, in Brian & Stewie... (If you don't, take a look and try to not puke.) That's friendship right there. In turn, who could fail to be touched by Stewie's heartfelt words to Brian, on life and death, in the same episode? These set out a sentiment we'll be seeing more of in Season 12:

Stewie: *"I like you a lot. I guess you could say I...really like you.
I would... even dare to go a little further, perhaps. I care a great deal about you. A very great deal.
Maybe even... deeper than that. I... I... [muffled] I love you. I mean, y'know, not in, like, a: "hey! Let's" – y'know – "let's have an underpants party!" Or, or, whatever grownups do when they're in love, but I mean, I mean: I love you.
As one loves another person whom one simply cannot do without."*

(Brian & Stewie)

BRIAN'S RÉSUMÉ

BRIAN GRIFFIN - WRITER

31 Spooner Street, Quahog, Rhode Island

During his short life, tortured creative soul Brian's written quite a body of work. In Season 12 he gets a big break (through a family connection), writing for teen detective show, Parent Boppers. So let's take this as an opportunity to look back at his literary life so far...

BOOKS

Faster Than the Speed of Love

"The story of a boy who has to rescue his father who is a pilot that's been taken captive by a militant Islamic country."

(Movin' Out (Brian's Song))

- Two million copies published

Wish It, Want It, Do It

"The steps necessary for identifying and achieving your dreams, and doing so in as effective and expeditious a manner as possible."

(Brian Writes a Bestseller)

- Published by "Penguin Group"
- Ranked at #3 on online bestseller list
- Featured on Quahog 5 News and Real Time with Bill Maher (with Arianna Huffington and Dana Gould)

Untitled Novel

About "a guy who loses everything, but finds his soul in Canada... The whole book is an email to his daughter who's dead...And his name will be Norm Hull. Because he's just a normal guy – but not everybody will get that, that's just for the scholars a hundred years from now."

(Stewie Goes for a Drive)

TELEVISION AND MOVIES

What I Learned on Jefferson Street

Television drama pilot, written as H. Brian Griffin

"Byron is a twenty-five-year-old single father going back to finish college, so he can do right by his four-year-old daughter."

Sample dialogue:

Byron: "Go ahead, Professor Watkins, fail me if you want. Give me an 'F' on the exam, I don't care because I got an 'A' today. As a dad. Maybe this is news to you, but love isn't some element on your periodic table – so you know what? Keep your chromium and magnesium, because I discovered a more precious element.

I discovered dad-mium."

(Brian Griffin's House of Payne)

- Produced as Class Holes!, starring James Woods.

Untitled

"Coming-of-age teen comedy set in Wisconsin."

(Brian Does Hollywood)

THEATRE

A Passing Fancy

Tragicomic local hit, nominated for a "Hoggy Award for Best Creative Anything."

Local newspaper review:

"Here's hoping A Passing Fancy is actually A Staying Fancy. The highest praise goes to playwright Brian Griffin for his hilarious and insightful look into modern relationships. If you see only one play as an adult, I urge you to see this one."

(Brian's Play)

OTHER WRITING

Brief stint at The New Yorker, plus reporting for publications including Teen People Magazine and The Quahog Daily Shopper

AWARDS

"Special Literary Excellence" (Dog Gone)

"New England's Rising Writer" (Play it Again, Brian)

EDUCATION

Seminar, New Haven

"Creating your own web-based internet series"

(Quagmire's Dad)

Brown University, Rhode Island - One class remaining

BRIAN ON WRITING

"Well, ysee, when I watch the world go by, I think of it kinda like a huge screen, yknow, every little interaction, every little moment is another scene captured by (he points to his head) this camera..."

(Quagmire's Dad)

"I think everybody has greatness in them, but it's really about having the courage to just kind of get inside your own head and just kind of poke around in there, yknow, and be like, hey, oh my gosh, what's under here? Hey! Whaddaya call yourself? Oh, wisdom. Oh! Profundity. Oh! Truth. Hey, Let's all just go hang out together, between the covers of a book."

(Brian Writes a Bestseller)

"It's overwhelming. This is all I've ever wanted, you know, for people to appreciate and respect my writing. "

(Brian's Play)

EVERYONE'S A CRITIC

"Worst-selling novel of all time"
Tom Tucker, Channel 5 News (Episode 420)

"Terrible writer"
Glen Quagmire (Jerome is the New Black)

"A little hackneyed and stilted"
Lois Griffin (Brian Does Hollywood)

"A mediocre patchwork of hackneyed ideas and tired clichés"
Stewie Gilligan Griffin (Brian's Play)

"Oh my god, what a load of rubbish! We have this thing where we go to the worst regional theatre we can find and laugh ourselves sick!"
Alan Bennett, Playwright (Brian's Play)

"You can't write"
Stewie Gilligan Griffin (Brian Writes a Bestseller)

STEWIE'S INSULT GENERATOR

If you really must insult people, you might as well be creative about it...Here are some classic, old-school Stewie barbs. Mix and match one from each column to create your own. But use them with caution, okay?

"YOU..."

Stewie's insults are put to very effective use – to beat Chris' bullies! – in brand new episode, Secondhand Spoke. Read more on page 67...

BROBDINGNAGIAN	BLUNDERBUSS (Mind Over Murder)
CONTEMPTIBLE	SHREW (Mind Over Murder)
DULL-WITTED	TERMAGANT (The Son Also Draws)
FESTERING	STRUMPET (Running Mates)
LOATHSOME	CUR (Running Mates)
BAWDY	LITTLE MONKEY (Running Mates)
GOURD-BELLIED	CODPIECE (The Story on Page One)
IDIOT	SLATTERN (Road to Rhode Island)
DRAGGLE-TAILED, BLUNT-EDGED	MATRIARCHAL DESPOT ((Back to the Pilot)
HOLIDAY	DRUNK (Brian Does Hollywood)
TOTTERING	FEN-SUCKED DEWBERRY (Lethal Weapons)
SICK, SICK	LITTLE MOO-COW (When You Wish Upon a Weinstein)
MEALY-MOUTHED	CROTCH-PHEASANT (From Method to Madness)
SACK-BELLIED	STRUMPET (From Method to Madness)
ATTENTION-GRABBING	JEZEBEL (From Method to Madness)

"Jeez. What'd you carry a thesaurus around with you?"

"You know, it's amazing I could speak at all with that circumcision still healing."

(Back to the Pilot)

You didn't have to wait as long for this as for Brian's first novel, but it's time your patience was rewarded. Get ready for emotional highs and lows, laughing, crying and puking. Oh, and some Quahog quotes that will impress all of your friends. Brian and Stewie have hit the headlines this time, so join us now as we take a sneaky peek at Season 12's adventures – no time machine required.

EPISODE 1: FINDERS KEEPERS

SEASON 12 EPISODE GUIDE

A Quahog Quest For Treasure…

Peter has terrible "Dad breath" and it's making everybody feel sick, so Lois sends him to the dentist. The cause is discovered, and to reward him for being well-behaved, Lois takes Peter and the family out for a meal at the Founding Father restaurant. Intrigued by the waiter's tales of Stewie's colour-in treasure map placemat, Peter leads his unconvinced family on a hunt for the loot, and soon they're in competition with the rest of Quahog's residents, to find it first…

WATCH OUT FOR:

- Peter's car radio sing-along.
- Stewie and Brian's hot air balloon trip.
- Tricia Takanawa as Lois.
- Peter using cutaway gag introductions to his own advantage…

PETER (TO LOIS): "LET'S DO SOME ROLE-PLAYIN'. YOU'RE YOU AND I'M PETER, ONLY WITH MUCH WORSE KNEES. (FAUX PAIN) OW, MY KNEES!"

EPISODE 2: VESTIGIAL PETER

SEASON 12 EPISODE GUIDE

Meet Peter's Tiny Twin...

Lois is sick of Peter wearing the same threadbare clothes, so takes him to the mall for a shopping spree. When he tries on a new shirt, but can't button it all the way up, they discover a lump on his neck, and Dr Hartman diagnoses a tiny "vestigial twin". He makes an incision to reveal an excitable chap, who Peter names Chip. Chip's wonder at the world endears him to the Griffins, but irritates the hell out of Peter, so Peter undertakes a risky operation to finally be free. Little does he know, Chip is about to save his neck (or, rather, his leg).

PETER: "THIS IS MY VESTIGIAL TWIN. I NAMED HIM 'CHIP'. YOU KNOW, LIKE 'CHIP OFF THE OLD NECK'. I LIKE TO POKE HIM BECAUSE IT MAKES HIM HAPPY AND I FEEL IT A LITTLE BIT IN MY NADS."

WATCH OUT FOR:

- Chip and the Griffins' theme song.
- Dr Hartman's post-surgery phonecall.
- Chip's first tennis match.
- Stewie's near-death instruction to Brian.

EPISODE 3: QUAGMIRE'S QUAGMIRE

SONJA: "GIGGITY"

QUAGMIRE (FRANTIC): "THAT'S MY WORD! THAT'S MY WORD!"

Glenn Discovers his Boundaries...

When Quagmire's new computer crashes, due to his dubious internet habits, he returns it to the store, only to find that Sonja in customer services shares his taste in websites. Their relationship develops quickly - and kinkily - and Quagmire is in love, but pretty soon he discovers that even he has his limits, and that Sonja's taking him way out of his comfort zone. It's not long before his friends realise that Quagmire is in serious trouble...

WATCH OUT FOR:

- The pedantic owl cutaway.
- Stewie's teddy bear love triangle.
- Peter's idea of a search mission.
- The Hawaiian shirt store.

EPISODE 4: A FISTFUL OF MEG

SEASON 12 EPISODE GUIDE

It's Time to Take on the School Psychopath...

There's a terrifying new kid at school, and it's just Meg's luck that she unwittingly lands in his bad books. He wants a fight and soon the whole school is talking about it. Meg is devastated, and totally scared, but Quagmire tells her he knows a thing or two about pushing the human body to its limits. If anyone can coach her to victory, he can. Meanwhile, Brian takes drastic action to stop a taunting, and very naked, Peter.

WATCH OUT FOR:

- Meg's birth certificate.
- Quagmire's "base of operations".
- The story of the 1980's "Cola Wars".

QUAGMIRE (TO MEG): "HE MAY BE STRONGER THAN YOU, BUT YOU'RE GROSSER."

EPISODE 5: BOOPA-DEE BAPPA-DEE

BRIAN (TO PETER): "...BEFORE YOU DO ANYTHING, FOR GOD'S SAKE PUT SOME CLOTHES ON."

PETER: "BRIAN, CALM DOWN. IN SOME COUNTRIES, THIS IS A COMPLIMENT."

Italian Family Guy

Low airfares convince Lois that it's time for the family to experience Europe, but Peter thinks they have all the culture they need in Quahog. So she buys the tickets to Italy anyway and tricks him onto a plane, hoping to put some Italian passion back into their stagnating lives. Her plan eventually works, and Peter gets into the spirit of things. In a grand romantic gesture, he throws the family's passports on the fire and declares that they will now live in Italy...

WATCH OUT FOR:

- Peter, Stewie and the TV remote.
- Meg's new boyfriend.
- Peter's football stadium message for Lois.
- Chris and the gondolier.

EPISODE 6: LIFE OF BRIAN

WATCH OUT FOR:

- Stewie's verdict on owning twin mattresses.
- The new addition to the family.
- Vinny's big "puke" question.

The Big Farewell…

Stewie has altered the past while time travelling, and he and Brian have another scarily close call putting right history, so, on their return home, Stewie decides that enough is enough and destroys his time machine. At the garbage dump, Brian spots a perfectly good street hockey net. The sport can take the place of time travel as their new hobby. But, when they set it up on Spooner Street, there is a terrible accident…

THIS EPISODE WAS WATCHED BY A TOTAL OF 4.58 MILLION PEOPLE!

STEWIE:
"DAMMIT, BRIAN, YOU CAN'T DIE. WE WERE GONNA DO SO MANY THINGS TOGETHER. WE WERE GONNA BECOME WINDSURFERS. I WAS GONNA BE A LITTLE BETTER THAN YOU, BUT WE WERE BOTH GONNA BE GOOD."

EPISODE 7: IN HARMONY'S WAY

PETER:

"NOW LET THIS BE A LESSON TO YOU, KIDS. IF YOU RANDOMLY STUMBLE UPON AN AMAZING TALENT, AND THEN SOMEONE IMPORTANT SEES IT BY WILD COINCIDENCE, GREAT THINGS CAN HAPPEN WITHOUT ANY HARD WORK."

Peter and Quagmire Make Sweet, Sweet Music Together

When a bee enters the Griffins' home, and Peter and Quagmire both yelp in fear, they realise their voices blend in perfect harmony. They're onto something good, but run out of paper whilst songwriting, so pop over to Mort Goldman's pharmacy to buy some more. Upon hearing their singing, Mort reveals that he used to run his own record label, "Mort Town", and convinces them to let him be their manager. A video Mort posts on "JewTube" gains attention, and a tour follows, but what is Peter's priority, music, or his family?

WATCH OUT FOR:

- 1970's Mort.
- Peter and Quagmire's songwriting talents.
- Their (Peter-approved) potential album covers.
- Quagmire's meditative chant.

EPISODE 8: CHRISTMAS GUY

SEASON 12 EPISODE GUIDE

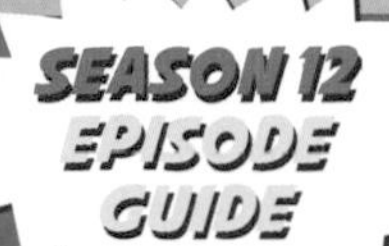

The Greatest Gift of All...

It's Stewie's "first Christmas" (again), and the Griffins head to Quahog Mall to get into the festive spirit, but the Christmas Carnival they'd been expecting has been cancelled. Stewie is devastated, and new dog Vinny discovers, through his contacts, that it's all down to the mall's owner, Carter Pewterschmidt. Peter works his magic on Carter, and eventually the festivities return to the mall. When Stewie sees Santa, he reveals the one thing missing in his life that would make his Christmas: Brian. Vinny takes Stewie to the toy store to cheer him up, and there he spots a familiar figure, who may have just what he needs to help rectify the past...

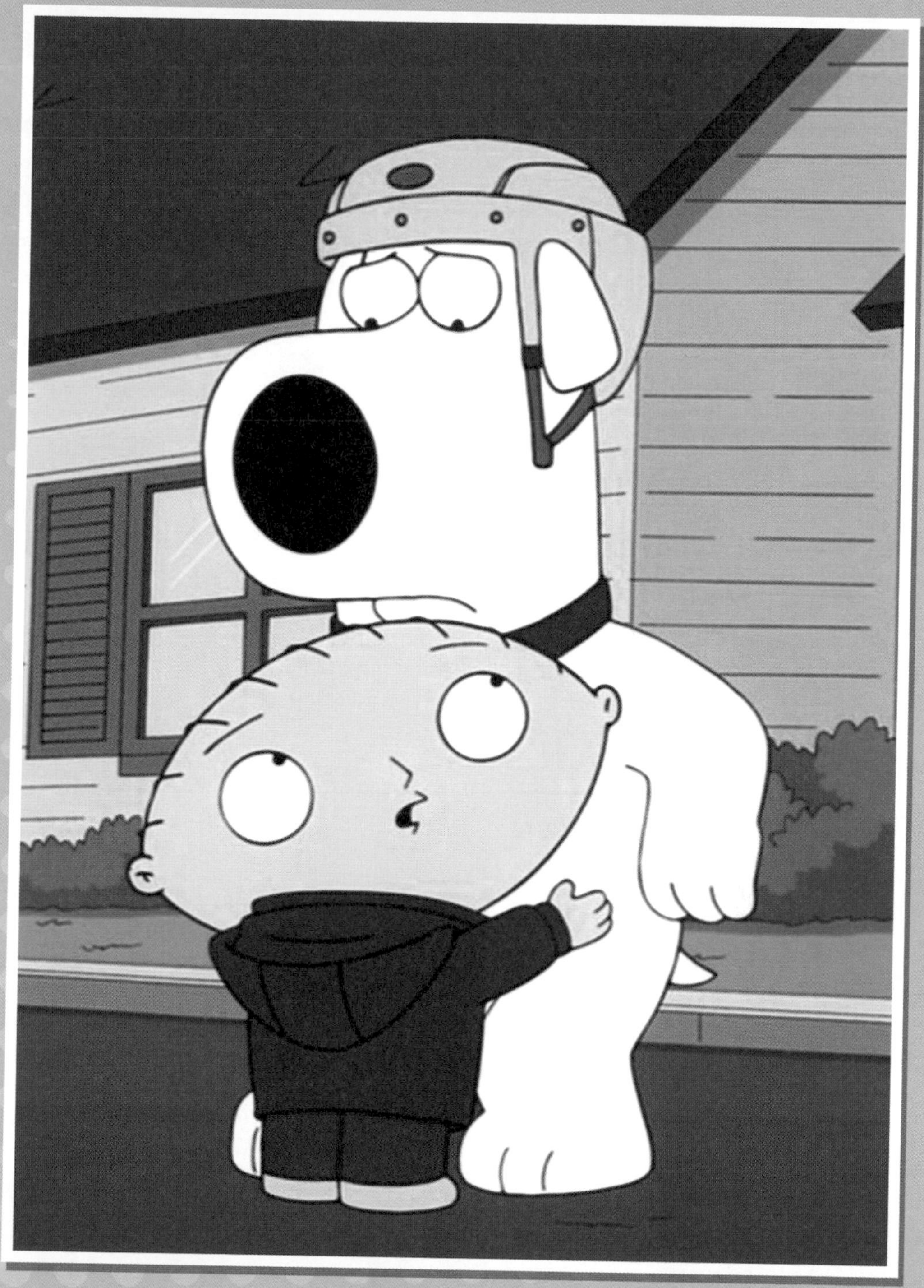

STEWIE:

"ALL I CAN SAY, BRIAN, IS YOU'VE BEEN MAKING REALLY CREEPY EYE CONTACT WITH ME ALL MORNING AND I WANT IT TO STOP RIGHT NOW."

WATCH OUT FOR:

- Peter's jewellery store chat.
- The eggnog incident.
- Vinny as 'Brian'.
- Stewie's 'model behaviour'.

EPISODE 9: PETER'S PROBLEMS

Peter Griffin: Man of the House

When Peter gets a promotion at work, he is overjoyed, and quickly begins to abuse his position. After a major incident involving a vast tank of beer and an executive boardroom, he is fired. It's hard for him to find a new job, so Lois decides that she will become the Griffin breadwinner, landing a position at the local "Stop N' Shop". Peter, meanwhile, takes on the difficult task of running their home. He takes pride in this, but the role reversal soon has troubling sexual consequences...

LOIS: "IT SEEMS LIKE YOU'VE REALLY TAKEN TO BEING A HOUSE-HUSBAND"

PETER: "WELL, IT HASN'T BEEN EASY. BETWEEN DOING THE LAUNDRY AND VACUUMING, I BARELY HAD TIME TO PUT ON A NICE SWEATER AND CLASP A CUP OF TEA WITH TWO HANDS."

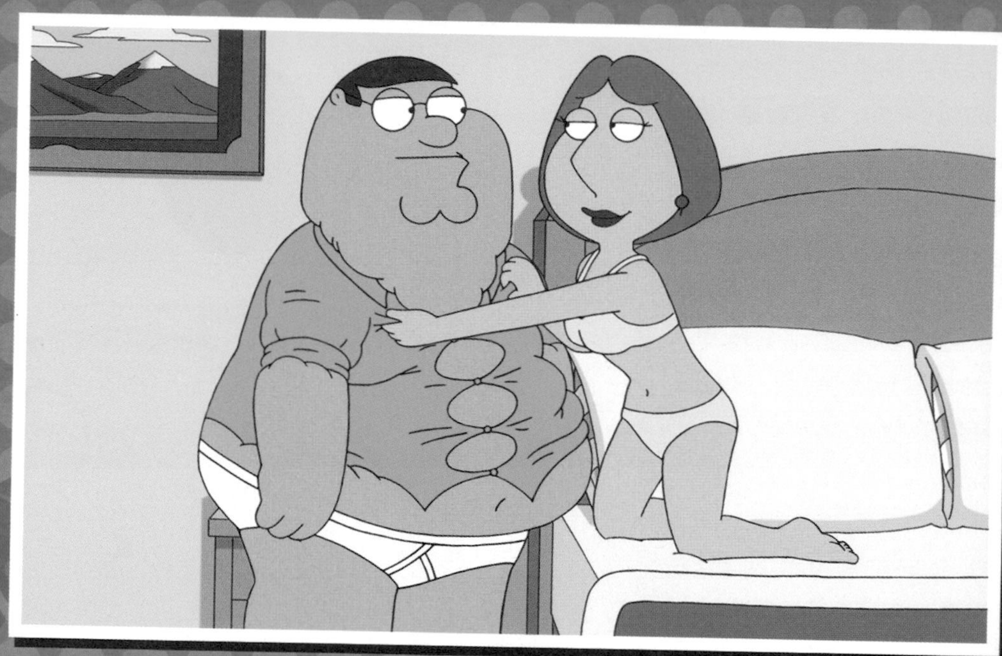

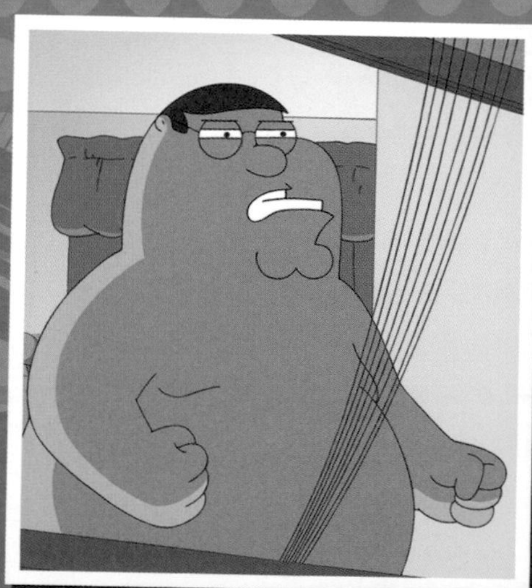

WATCH OUT FOR:

- The elaborate promotion "cutaway setup".
- Peter's podcast.
- The scene with Dr Hartman.

EPISODE 10: GRIMM JOB

Once Upon a Time...

One night, Peter checks on Stewie, and decides to read him a story (whether he likes it or not). Cue fairytale adventures, featuring some familiar Family Guy faces, as Peter becomes Jack (of that beanstalk fame), Stewie dons the cape as Little Red Riding Hood, and Lois gets the fairy godmother treatment, as the careless shoe-loser, Cinderella.

PETER: "I GOT THIS GOLDEN GOOSE! OUR TROUBLES ARE OVER! (THEN) WELL, OUR – OUR MONEY TROUBLES ARE OVER. OUR SEXUAL TROUBLES ARE STILL – ARE STILL VERY MUCH ALIVE..."

WATCH OUT FOR:

- Quagmire and "Little Miss Muffet" (and her "tuffet").
- The "cool whip" callback.
- Fairy Godmother, Mayor West.
- The "happily ever after".

EPISODE 11: BRIAN'S A BAD FATHER

BRIAN:
"YEAH, I-I DECIDED TO STEP AWAY FROM THE WHOLE SITUATION. THE LAST THING HE NEEDS IS A FATHER WHO'S, YOU KNOW, SOMETIMES THERE, SOMETIMES NOT."

Don't Work with (Your Estranged) Children or (Talking, Writing) Animals.

Brian's son Dylan is back in town, and Brian's doing all he can to avoid him – until he hears that Dylan landed a lead role on new TV teen detective show, 'Parent Boppers'. Eager to get a writing gig on it, Brian summons up all the dad-ly charm he can muster. But, once he's on the show, his writing causes problems, and Dylan quickly realises the truth…

WATCH OUT FOR:

- Brian's "magic typewriter" idea.
- The lion cub cutaway.
- Stewie's "audition" (as Zac Sawyer).
- The Stewie/cab driver exchange.

EPISODE 12: MOM'S THE WORD

When Grief Gets Awkward…

Raw cookie dough, an upset stomach and a long and quiet meeting result in embarrassment for Peter, who soils his pants at work. When he returns home, shame-faced, there's a welcoming committee, and Peter learns his mother, Thelma, has died. The family visits her apartment, where Peter meets Evelyn, Thelma's good friend, and they quickly form a bond. But Evelyn has more than friendship in mind…

BRIAN:

"LOOK, STEWIE, I KNOW YOU'RE WORRIED, BUT YOU CAN'T LIVE YOUR LIFE BEING SCARED OF DEATH. NOBODY KNOWS WHAT COMES NEXT, SO ALL WE CAN DO IS PACK THE MOST WE CAN INTO EACH DAY WE'VE GOT."

WATCH OUT FOR:

- Confession-mode Peter.
- Peter's "vaguebooking".
- Joe's Drunken Clam miracle.
- Stewie's superhero alter ego.

EPISODE 13: FRESH HEIR

WATCH OUT FOR:

- Babs Pewterschmidt's magazine cover shoot.
- Lois' 'dramatic' new haircut.
- Chris teaching an old man a new trick…
- Peter's "too many steps to remember" handshake.

For Richer, for Poorer – But Mainly for Richer...

Chris is desperate to spend some quality father-son time with Peter, but unless Chris is the TV or internet, Peter's having none of it. So, when Carter breaks his leg and nobody else is around to help him, Chris takes on the job. They have an excellent time together, and Carter is taken aback that his grandson wants no payment for it, so decides to leave everything to him in his will. Peter is somewhat put out, but he has a plan…

LOIS: "PETER... DID YOU MARRY ME FOR MY MONEY?"

PETER: "OF COURSE NOT, LOIS. BUT EVEN YOU CAN'T DENY IT WAS ALWAYS GONNA BE A HUGE PERK. (THEN) D-DID I USE THAT RIGHT, "PERK"?"

LOIS: "YES, PETER"

EPISODE 14: SECONDHAND SPOKE

Work is a Drag, and School Needs a Bag...

When Peter realises his colleague Stella's cigarette breaks go unchallenged by their boss, he immediately takes up the habit - using it as an excuse to get out of any undesirable activity, at work and at home. But smoking has consequences, as Peter soon discovers – pity, then, that he is now addicted. Meanwhile, Stewie steps in to help his bullied big brother – boosting Chris' popularity in the process - but soon the bullied becomes the bully.

STEWIE: "DAY FIVE OF MY IMPRISONMENT INSIDE CHRIS' BACKPACK. FAECES, AND THE BUILDUP THEREOF, CONTINUES TO BE MY NUMBER ONE PROBLEM. I THINK A TEACHER SAW ME THE OTHER DAY BUT SAID NOTHING. I WAVED AND HE LOOKED AWAY."

WATCH OUT FOR:

- Chris' geometry test answer.
- Stewie's time-honoured insults.
- Principal Shepherd's school announcements.
- Peter's ad campaign.

EPISODE 15: BLOOD BROTHERS

Stewie is intrigued by the idea of becoming blood brothers with Brian, who finally agrees to it. But the next morning, Stewie discovers a horrible sore on his lip and realises he's contracted herpes. Brian, it transpires, is riddled with disease, and when Stewie and Chris learn that they have both suffered the same fate, they plot revenge on Brian's love life. Meanwhile, Peter and the guys must take action to reclaim their regular spot at the Clam – and their reputations.

STEWIE:
"BRIAN, I WANT YOU INSIDE ME."

BRIAN:
"YOU – YOU DON'T HAVE TO SAY IT LIKE THAT."

WATCH OUT FOR:

- Another "cool whip" callback.
- Brian's new profile picture.
- Stewie's most recent Halloween costume.

EPISODE 16: THE MOST INTERESTING MAN IN THE WORLD

Books Are the New TV...

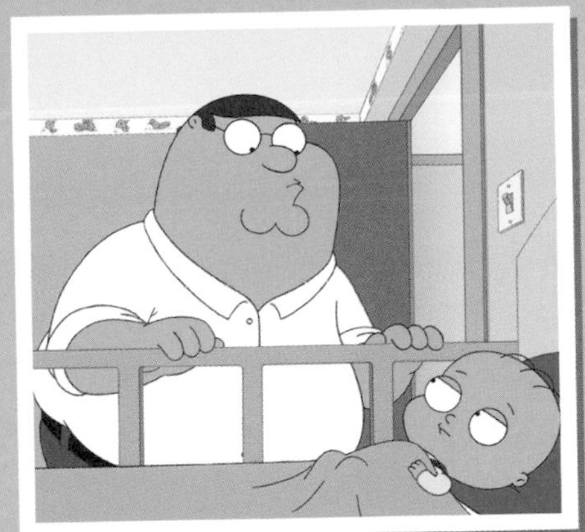

When Peter is left in charge of Stewie and returns home with the wrong baby, Lois calls him an idiot. He's depressed and hurt and opens up to Quagmire and Joe, who tell him he should broaden his horizons. An opportunity to travel comes up at work so Peter grabs it, soaking up as much culture as possible on his trips. Pretty soon Peter is unrecognisable – and the rest of the family are not sure they like it...

PETER:
"I LIVE THE LIFE OF THE MIND NOW. MY BRAIN IS AWASH WITH THEOREMS AND PROFUNDITY AND ABSTRACTIONS THAT I CAN PONTIFICATE UPON AT LENGTH."

WATCH OUT FOR:

- Peter's Chicago museum trip.
- Peter's new smart glasses.
- Brian and Peter discussing literature.

EPISODE 17: BABY GOT BLACK

Chris Gets a Girlfriend – But Not Everyone's Happy...

Peter wins two hundred dollars in a "staying awake" competition, so the family head out for a fancy meal. While Chris is choosing which lobster he'd like to die, he runs into Jerome's daughter, Pam, who expresses her interest in him. Jerome has serious reservations about her dating Chris, so the now-couple run away. As the dads track them down, Peter finds out why Jerome has such a problem with the relationship.

WATCH OUT FOR:

- Peter, Joe and Quagmire's sleep-deprived hallucinations.
- The lobster chat.
- Chris and Pam's motel companion.
- Peter's homage to a 1980's movie classic.

BRIAN:
"IT'S ABOUT TIME PEOPLE OF COLOUR BROKE BREAD AT THIS TABLE."

STEWIE:
"BROKE BREAD"? W-W-WHO ARE YOU, ST. FRANCIS OF ASSISI ALL OF A SUDDEN?"

EPISODE 18: MEG STINKS!

**PETER:
"OH, MEG! THERE YOU ARE! LET'S PUT ON FAKE EYE LASHES AND FLIRT WITH PEOPLE ON THE BUS."**

Meg and Peter: the Whiff of Friendship…

When Meg's top-choice college invites her for an interview, it's dad-daughter road trip time, and she finally gets to the bottom of his feelings towards her. As newly-bonded pals, Peter leads Meg on an exhausting path of juvenile escapades, and a big decision looms. Meanwhile, a very smelly Brian must fend for himself in the Great Outdoors…

WATCH OUT FOR:

- Peter's original career aspirations.
- "Scrappy Brian".
- Peter's piercing…
- Brian's skunk confrontation.

EPISODE 19: HE'S BLA-ACK!

SEASON 12 EPISODE GUIDE

Cleveland Returns…

Stoolbend's loss is Quahog's gain, as the Browns return to Spooner Street - and their now-wreck-of-a-house. The Drunken Clammers are reunited, but it's not long before neighbourly tensions rise and Peter and Cleveland are forbidden from spending time together. Cue illicit rendezvous - and ruses to bond their warring wives…

PETER (TO CLEVELAND): "HERE'S FOUR SEASONS WORTH OF DVDS OF WHAT WE'VE BEEN UP TO. JUST SO, YOU KNOW, YOU'RE BACK UP TO SPEED. AND I'LL WARN YOU AHEAD OF TIME, THESE HAVE JOKES IN 'EM."

WATCH OUT FOR:

- Cleveland's 'showstopping' main-titles entrance.
- Stewie versus Rallo – is this town big enough for both babies?
- Susie Swanson's first birthday. Seven years in the womb – she's growing up fast!
- Joe's toes…

HELLO, CLEVELAND!

HE'S BEEN TO STOOLBEND AND BACK...

That familiar laugh is about to grip Rhode Island once more, after four whole seasons in Virginia.

Quahog is calling Cleveland Brown, as his old life beckons... But he no longer has just Cleveland Junior in tow - there's his whole new family, ready to make Spooner Street their home. So how will his glamorous, no-nonsense wife, Donna Tubbs-Brown, take to the place – and to Lois – after their dodgy start? And, perhaps more to the point, how will Cleveland's step-children, Roberta and Rallo Tubbs, fit in with Meg, Chris and Stewie? It's going to be fun finding out...

Talking of 'tubs', here's hoping Cleveland's former residence is structurally sound, what with all those bathtub incidents (see what we did there?). And, here's hoping that it doesn't need fumigating; we know that Peter took all of his dumps in his empty neighbourly abode, before Dan Ackroyd and Chevy Chase finally moved in, in Spies Reminiscent of Us. We'd like to think that Ryan Reynolds did some work on the place during his tenancy, in Stewie Goes for a Drive, but that would be mere speculation. (Plus, he was possibly too busy filming his movie, 'Hotler'. And obsessing about Peter.)

Don't expect the guys to let Cleveland off lightly for daring to leave them – and for coming back. He's in for some serious ribbing. This was all predicted in Back to the Pilot, when Stewie time-travels five years into the future, spots Cleveland, and says, "ugh, I guess things didn't work out in Virginia." Ever wise, Stewie, ever wise.

And, after events with ex-wife, Loretta, it seems likely that Cleveland will be keeping an eye on Quagmire (or he'll be completely oblivious, one of the two...). We can't imagine Donna would ever fall for Quagmire's ways, but stranger things have happened in Quahog...

EPISODE 20: CHAP STEWIE

If Stewie Really Were British…

The Griffins are morons… is the conclusion Stewie comes to, when their doofus antics prevent him from watching his favourite British television show, 'The Cadwalliders of Essex'. The moment has arrived to get back in the time-travel game, to prevent his own birth. But Stewie's dream is about to become a nightmare, when he's reborn - as an actual Brit…

WATCH OUT FOR:

- A selection of imaginatively-titled 'British' television shows.
- The reason Brian started drinking.
- How Peter spent his days before Stewie was born.
- Chris' three-year hobby.

STEWIE: "I LOATHE THIS FAMILY! BEING BORN INTO IT WAS CLEARLY SOME SORT OF COSMIC MISTAKE, SO I'M GOING BACK IN TIME TO PREVENT THAT MISTAKE. I'M GOING TO BREAK UP LOIS AND THE FAT MAN BEFORE THEY CAN CONCEIVE ME."

EPISODE 21: 3 ACTS OF GOD

Peter Worships the Patriots...

When Peter's team lose their football game – again – and the opposition thank God – again – Peter concludes that God must hate his team. He vows to find God and tell him to stop ruining their Sundays, leading the guys on a fruitless worldwide search. Back at the Clam, Death arrives and agrees to take them to God, in Heaven - who sets them a task...

WATCH OUT FOR:

- Peter's university montage.
- Death coming for Cleveland's show.
- The cutaway gag about cutaway gags...
- Heaven – Family Guy-style.

GOD:
"...WE DON'T PROVIDE TOWELS; YOU HAVE TO BRING YOUR OWN. IT'S VERY IMPORTANT THAT YOU DIE HOLDING TOWELS. HAVE THE PRIESTS NOT BEEN PASSING THIS ALONG? IT'S VERY IMPORTANT."

EPISODE 22: BAKING BAD

Peter Dreams Up a Scheme to Bring in the Dough...

Lois organises a charity blood drive and lures Peter to donate with the promise of a homemade cookie. Impressed, Peter convinces Lois that they should run a business together, so they sweet-talk the bank into lending them money and open a cookie store. Trade is slow, so Peter gets inventive, taking heed of Quagmire's advice that "sex sells". Meanwhile, Stewie discovers a 'cure' for his insomnia...

PETER:
"WELL, I ALREADY ATE TWO WEDDING CAKES, BUT I GUESS I COULD GO FOR A COOKIE. ALRIGHT, I'LL DO IT."

WATCH OUT FOR:

- The cookie-sample-taking woman.
- Stewie's intervention.
- Dr Hartman's mum.

The time has come to say goodbye for another year.

If this is too sad to bear, glance fondly at your newly-acquired butt scratcher (or maybe even use it); make another batch of 'Rocky Road To...' bars and relive the adventures; shoehorn a Chris quote into everyday conversation; create your own Stewie-style insults using the best generator of all (your brain); or just rejoice in that feeling of sweet relief that you aren't Meg and that those mortifying moments have NEVER happened to you.

After the events of Season 12, who knows exactly what's in store for the Griffins next. All we know is we're never taking any of them for granted ever again. Hold your nearest and dearest close, and take care.

Until next time...

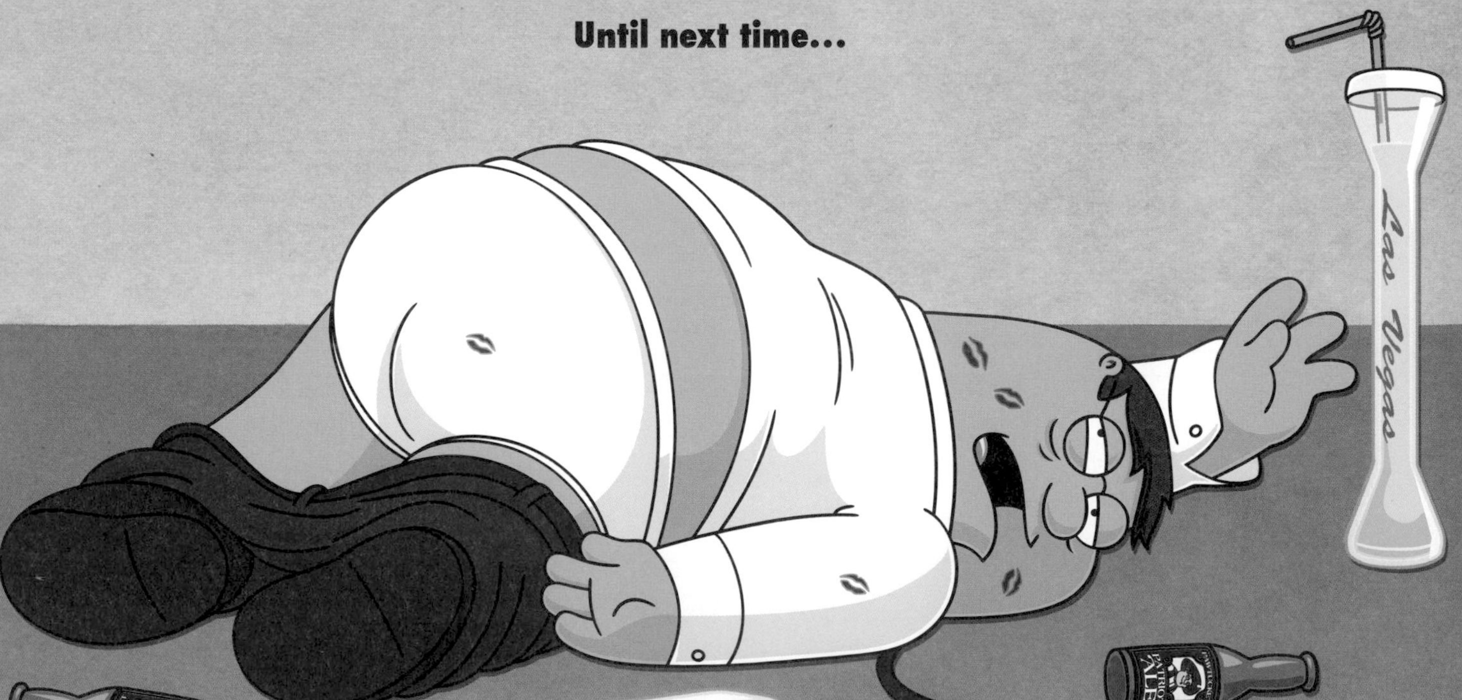

PAGE 42 – The Family Guy Hit Parade

1 Booze (Friends of Peter G.)
2 Fries (Deep Throats)
3 Song (Road to Rupert)
4 Toad (Let's Go to the Hop!)
5 House (Peter, Peter, Caviar Eater)
6 Fingernails (The Giggity Wife)
7 Baby (Airport '07)
8 Weed (Episode 420)
9 See (Brian Wallows and Peter's Swallows)
10 Intercourse (Don't Make Me Over)
11 Irish (Peter's Two Dads)
12 Pie (Road to the Multiverse)
13 Awfully (Road to Europe)
14 Nude (You May Now Kiss the... Uh... Guy Who Receives)
15 Lesson (Brian Wallows and Peter's Swallows)
16 Friendship (Hannah Banana)
17 Touch (E. Peterbus Unum)
18 Bigoted (Jerome is the New Black)
19 Fat (To Love and Die in Dixie)
20 Do (From Method to Madness)

PAGE 44 – The Big Quahog Quiz

1 Hollywood actor
2 Cherrywood Manor
3 Newport Country Club
4 Towel Boy
5 The Real Live Griffins
6 Lando Griffin
7 Mr Nubbins
8 Stewie
9 Handi-Quacks
10 Poopyface Tomatonose and Red Hiney Monkey
11 Xerxes
12 Patrice
13 Glenda Vagmire
14 Kent

PAGE 40 – The Ultimate Episode Crossword

1 AHEROSITSNEXTDOOR
2 THEBIGBANGTHEORY
3 PADREDEFAMILIA
4 THEPERFECTCASTAWAY
5 THESPLENDIDSOURCE
6 QUAGMIRESDAD
7 IDREAMOFJESUS
8 DEEPTHROATS
9 PETERPETERCAVIAREATER
10 BARELYLEGAL
11 THEGRIFFINFAMILYHISTORY
12 BRIANWRITESABESTSELLER

15 Sheldon
16 McBurgertown
17 Martin Mull Elementary
18 pLace (Stewie: "Little 'p', big 'L'")
19 Harmonica
20 He plays it with his butt
21 The Barrington Country Club
22 Principessa
23 Patrick Stewart
24 Todd
25 15
26 Carol
27 Mayor West
28 Patrick
29 Joe Swansonson
30 Daniel "Dan" Quagmire
31 Oscar
32 His grandparents, the Pewterschmidts
33 Jesse
34 Mike Henry
35 Franz Gutentag
36 Carl
37 Alex Borstein
38 Connie D'Amico
39 Thelma Griffin
40 Mittens
41 Mrs Lockhart
42 Brian's son
43 Jolly Farm Revue
44 London
45 Charles Dickens
46 Jake
47 Kevin
48 1984
49 He asks Death to take him
50 Miles "Chatterbox" Musket

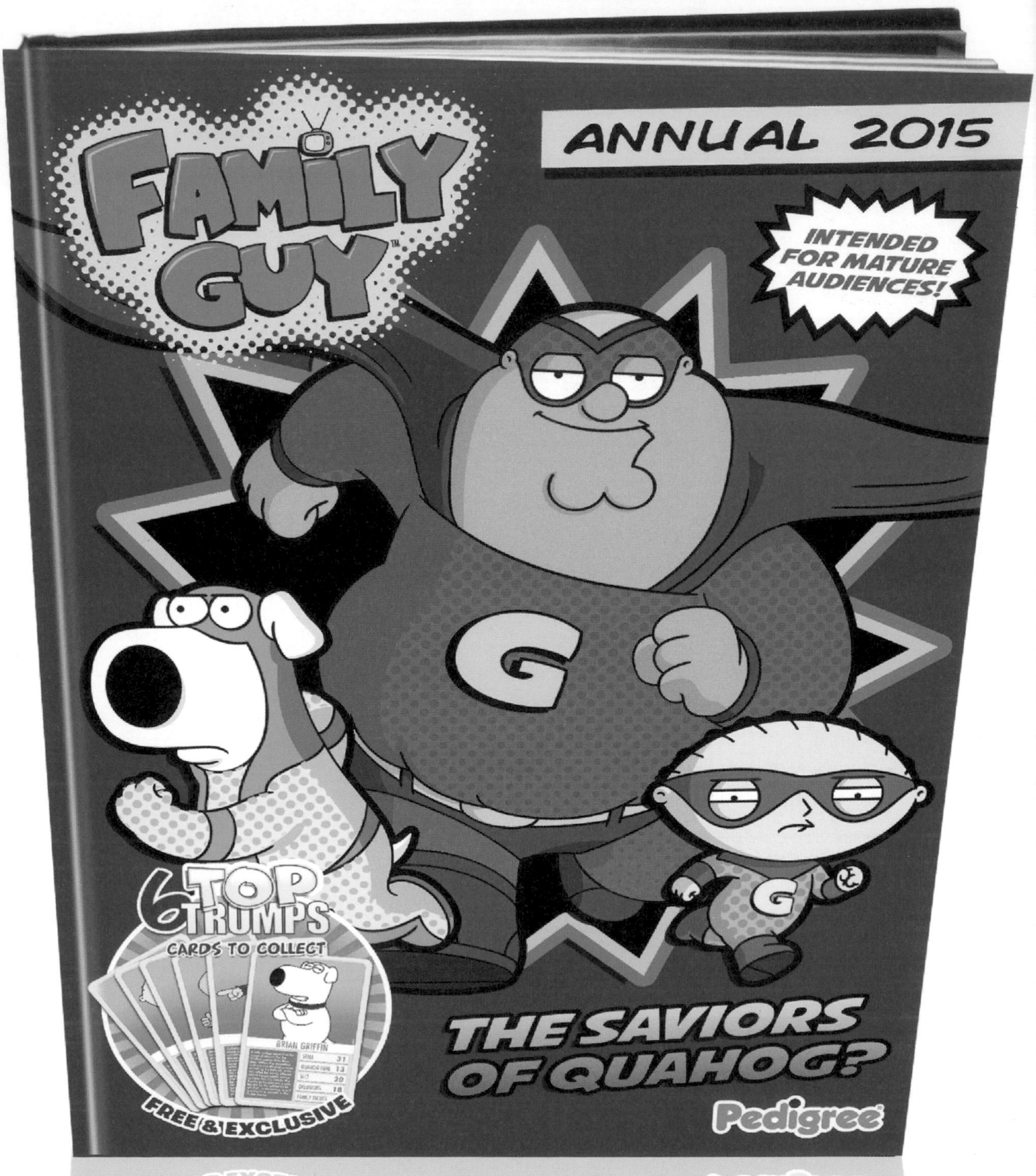